Sartre

THE
RADICAL
CONVERSION

Sartre

THE
RADICAL
CONVERSION

JAMES F. SHERIDAN, JR.

OHIO UNIVERSITY PRESS
ATHENS, OHIO

To my mother and father
who gave so much
and asked so little.

Preface

When I began to concentrate upon the later thought of Jean-Paul Sartre, I was intrigued by the periodic appearance of the claim that his latest major work, *Critique de la Raison Dialectique*, was a betrayal of the existentialism which he had earlier espoused. The only part of the *Critique* which I had then read was Hazel Barnes' translation of the introduction and I could not substantiate these objections by reference to that work. I assumed that the charge must be based upon the remainder of the *Critique* and that I should discover its sources once I began to go through the rest of the book. In the interim, however, I was reading various other late essays by Sartre and I could find nothing sufficiently different from the earlier position to certify the charge of betrayal. The more I read, the more it seemed to me that Sartre's critics were selecting themes from some of his total output and simply neglecting themes in other writings which were inconsistent with the portrait which they had formed of him. The mere fact of selection did not disturb me, for, with the volume of pages Sartre has turned out, selection was neither avoidable nor undesirable. There was also the fact that *Being and Nothingness*, the capstone of his early efforts, was available in English while the *Critique* was not wholly translated. But I was puzzled enough to go back to *Being and Nothingness* to read some of the passages cited by Sartre's detractors and to look for passages which memory suggested made their charge much less plausible.

While I was engaged in this labor, Odajnyk's book, *Marxism and Existentialism*, came into my possession, and this time the repetition of the charge of betrayal infuriated me. I wrote a review of Odajnyk which I reproduce in part below. I now think that I was slightly unfair to him because I was speaking to Sartre's detractors in general as much as to the book itself, but I have not changed my opinion of the conclusion I announced nor of the task I recommended:

Odajnyk concludes that Sartre has failed to achieve an integration of existentialism and Marxism, and has abandoned the former for the latter. But it is not clear that Sartre ever needed to seek an integration and much less clear that he has abandoned the views announced in *Being and Nothingness*. Sartre still insists that his "existentialism" is opposed only to an "idealistic" Marxism, that his views do and must occur in our Marxist situation. There are also rather obvious connections among the notions of *pour-soi* and *en-soi*, being-in-a-situation, and the predicted demise of Marxism when our situation has become one of real freedom. But, until Odajnyk provides the missing analyses of Sartre, one cannot fairly assess this puzzling neglect of Sartre's claims.

When Warnock's version of this charge appeared, I wrote a similar review and I considered briefly whether I should provide some of the analyses I had recommended to Odajnyk as an adjunct, but, before I had decided, it occurred to me that perhaps I should take my own recommendations more seriously. I had done that once in a piece accepted by the *Journal of Existentialism* in which I had used material from the Barnes trans-

viii

lation. As I became progressively engrossed in the *Critique*, it became obvious that the selection of topics with which I was concerned all bore upon the charge which had so offended me. I then decided that I could speak to it without abandoning my continuing study of Sartre if I made the bearing of each topic upon the charge explicit.

This book is the result of these considerations. The introduction is a combination of my abortive review of Warnock and the piece I had done out of *Search for a Method*. While Warnock's objections are by no means the most careful among those available in English, her work clearly shows the content and tone of the charge that Sartre's thought has undergone a radical conversion. The first third of the introduction exhibits her statement of this contention and some obvious counterevidence. The rest of this piece provides an abrupt rebuttal to Warnock through the development of a crucial passage from *Search for a Method* in which Sartre explicitly relates his later work to a fundamental theme in *Being and Nothingness* and simultaneously refuses the variety of Marxism which Warnock appears to attribute to him. This confrontation is intended to be brutal rather than careful. It is intended to raise the question forcefully, and willingly pays the penalty of the introduction of themes which require much explicit development if their philosophic impact is to be fully assessed.

The first chapter presents partial expositions of two of Sartre's "popular" articles, "Existentialism is a Humanism" and "Materialism and Revolution," treating the first as an expression of the philosophizing done in *Being and Nothingness* and the second as a precursor of a line of thought which eventually came to culmination in the *Critique de la Raison Dialectique*. This effort is intended to set the issue of the radical conversion in a relatively restricted context, thus providing an overview. In addition, the popular character of the first article provides an example of the style which is partly responsible for a mistaken reading of Sartre's early views. The second chapter is written to provide a correction for that reading by emphasizing some of the restrictions upon freedom which are presented in *Being and Nothingness*. This emphasis is deliberately an overemphasis through the selection of the "restrictive" aspects. It is intended to counteract the overstatement of Sartre's views on freedom which have resulted from a different selection of thematic material, the selection made by Warnock, for instance.

The last four essays develop these themes in the context of the *Critique*. The third essay brings some of them to a focus familiar to analytically oriented readers through the consideration of Sartre's conceptions as they apply to the formal disciplines, in this case to geometry. Since the term "formalist" signalizes an attitude now held by many toward reasoning in mathematics and logic, the intent of the essay is to provide access to Sartre's categories in a familiar nonsartrean framework. Because the chapter is set in this heterogeneous context, what is required next is a sustained account of the relationship of dialectical and analytical reason in Sartre's own terms. The fourth chapter begins that process by beginning at Sartre's "beginning," the portion of the *Critique* devoted to individual *praxis*. This is perhaps the most academic of the essays and is also placed where it is, in order to provide a literal ground for the liberties taken with Sartrean language in the succeeding pieces. For instance, the chapter concludes with some of Sartre's discussion of the notion of reciprocity, and the next essay is concerned with an extension of that discussion in terms of chess. But I then take the liberty of using chess not only as an illustration for *réciprocité antagonistique* but also as an illustration of some of the other themes discussed thus far and of themes not yet explicitly considered.

This consideration of chess suggested to me that one might well give further consideration to the varieties of reason in terms of the "game metaphor" which is currently in vogue among Anglo-Saxon philosophers. The sixth piece does that. It argues that the application of that metaphor is inappropriate chiefly because it will not account for Sartre's claim that dialectical reason necessarily becomes analytical reason. Because that necessity is not exhibited, it is easy to miss the fact that dialectical necessity is not only consistent with human freedom but actually requires precisely the radical view of human freedom which Sartre has always held. The last piece underscores this contention by using materials from Sartre's early period and draws support from Sartre's friend and critic, Maurice Merleau-Ponty.

Although the sequence of the chapters is designed to be developmental, no pretense is made that the series is not due to "reading backwards" from the *Critique*. This is particularly true of the first two essays. The fact that I make this comment is evidence enough of my unease. At first I was able to comfort myself with the notion that I was engaged in a *totalization* in which case I could do no other than to begin at the end. But that attitude was all too schematic for my taste and, in addition, it might commit me to the claim that my work was itself dialectical, a possibility which I do not wish to entertain until I have finished my second manuscript, a study of Sartre and Merleau-Ponty. When I finished this book, however, I realized that what I had done was to begin in a portion of an ambiguous domain and make it more definite just as had Sartre's detractors. But I had also learned again that, while there is no such thing as *the* interpretation in philosophy, not every interpretation is equally admissible. What this book represents is an effort which it is hoped will blunt the edge of the criticism I condemn and suggest further lines of investigation of the later work of Jean-Paul Sartre.

To try to acknowledge all of the assistance I have had in preparing this volume would be an endless task, so I shall restrict myself to the bare minimum. To William Linden, Chairman of the Humanities Division at Southern Illinois University at Edwardsville, Illinois, I owe thanks for the combination of friendship and professional commitment which forced me to consider whether my previous refusal to write had been lengthy enough to indicate incapacity rather than stubborness. To Professor Alfred Kern, Chairman of the English department at Allegheny College, I owe a debt which defies repayment, for personal and professional support as generous as it was undemanding. I am in debt to my wife, Nancy, for proofing, typing, criticism and just for being my wife. I am indebted to Allegheny College for continuing financial assistance in many different forms. I should like to thank Random House for permission to quote and translate passages from Jean-Paul Sartre, *Critique de la Raison Dialectique* (Gallimard: 1960). Finally, I happily express my gratitude to the staff of Ohio University Press for their seemingly inexhaustible patience with the vagaries of a new author.

Contents

Introduction

The claim that Sartre's later work is sharply inconsistent with his earlier efforts has been asserted by a variety of his English commentators including Walter Odajnyk, Wilfrid Desan, and Mary Warnock. One is hesitant to contest authorities of this stature, yet the evidence against their contention is both formidable and readily available. Since our chief effort in the body of this book is to combat that claim and to offer an alternative interpretation, it is well to introduce that effort by selecting a strong statement of the opinion we oppose and indicating some of the most obvious of the counter-evidence. For this purpose, we select from Warnock's *The Philosophy of Sartre* the following unequivocal statement of the view that Sartre's latest work constitutes an abandonment of his existentialism:

Sartre, at the end of *Being and Nothingness*, promised a book on ethics. What he wrote, in fact, was a book on sociology. . . . He has succeeded in rendering his thought, and the style of his writing, still more abstract and obscure than it was in *Being and Nothingness*. Whether anything has been gained to compensate for the loss of concreteness and insight is less clear. Indeed, it must be admitted that it is a depressing task to analyse this latest book, as much as we have of it; for in it we see the spectacle of the death of Sartrean existentialism, . . . It cannot be understood except as an attempt to justify the conversion hinted at in *Being and Nothingness*. It is a deliberate rejection of the individual.[1]

The tone and content of Warnock's language is surprisingly adamant, but the type of evidence she offers is even more surprising. She begins, for example, with one of the oldest and most worn of polemical devices—what Sartre says has been said before, in this case, by Thomas Hobbes. She then cites some of Hobbes' difficulties and, through guilt by association, assigns them to Sartre. She asserts—with little provision of evidence—that Hobbes, Sartre, and dialectical materialists in general have a priori systems, systems which have little or no basis in experience much less being founded upon inferences from experience. Apparently she believes that any such system must force historical events into its pattern, and Sartre's does "perhaps inevitably." Even if one accepted this presumed consequence of the possession of an a priori system, one would like to see in somewhat more concrete terms just how Sartre does what apparently this philosopher of freedom must do!

Warnock's criticism continues with further reference to the supposed similarity of the views of Sartre and Hobbes. This time she asserts that both posit "one unified society" as the goal of a social or political process. Despite her assertion that the notion of a totality is never clearly formulated by Sartre, she finds it clear enough to equate with the notion of one unified society. A doleful consequence of the achievement of such a group is the establishment of a kind of identity between one person and another. This totalization strikes her as "sinister" and seems to her to amount to the "suppression of individual liberty." In a setting so lacking in detailed analysis or argument there is little motivation to see Warnock's comments as any-

2

thing other than her own psychological responses to Sartre and thus hard to weigh their philosophic import. It is even more difficult to take her remarks seriously when they obviously ignore features of Sartre's thought to which Warnock herself has called attention. For example, she grants correctly that totalization is always an individual act and thus that the presumed identification of individuals with each other does not make them any less individuals because they participate in a totalization. On the other hand, she neglects features of Sartre's position at least as obvious as those she cites. She neglects, for instance, Sartre's careful account of the ossification of an institution, of its degeneration into a *pratique petrifée*. Sartre's account of this development could scarcely support a "sinister" characterization of the group except to one like Warnock who endorses "some vaguely liberal situation which we may feel we should prefer." Further illustration of her curious evaluative procedures is unnecessary. One need only cite one of her concluding remarks:

It is true that we are told in the *Critique* that the group is not an organic unity, that its existence is the existence of the individuals which compose it, viewed in a certain light. We are told, further, that the concept of the group-in-fusion cannot be intelligibly described except in terms of the individual effect on the outside world of individual praxis, and that the *a priori* foundation of Marxist theory is to be found in this individual praxis. But, unfortunately, merely saying that two things are compatible does not make them so; and there remains a fundamental and unbridgeable gap between the goal of the dialectical development of the group, and the world of individual projects to which we were introduced in *Being and Nothingness*.[2]

Nor does saying that a thing is not so make it not so. As all of us once heard from our major professor in graduate school, "If this is worth saying, it is worth arguing."

Perhaps the kindest treatment which we could accord to this "criticism" would be to suppose that Warnock is rehearsing minor objections as a prelude to the presentation of the kind of

3

acute criticism of which she is eminently capable. That technique is not unknown among many of her cohorts in England and in this country. If nothing else, it has persuasive value, for the position thus attacked appears to be weakened by a barrage of trivia even if no one of the barbs is expected to be destructive. But surely a philosopher of Warnock's competence would not be content with mere sniping. One breathlessly anticipates the coup de grace but it is never delivered. What one finds is more of the same kind of assault used to advance the claim that the "failure" of the *Critique* to be an ethics was inevitable given the standpoint of *Being and Nothingness*, ". . . the private, compelling myth of the free man, experiencing his freedom in anguish and faced with no necessity except that of choosing himself." What is worse, she says, even this notion of "an intuited personal freedom with which Sartre's existentialism begins and ends" has been abandoned for the poor sociology of the *Critique*. I suggest that these two quotations give us the clue to understanding why Warnock did not proceed to the delivering of a fatal blow. With many others, she has confused the impression left by Sartre's literary works, the position of a sort of Gallic Ayn Rand, with the statement of human freedom in *Being and Nothingness*. The result is an overstatement of the radical character of Sartre's conception of freedom. After all, the Other did function in *Being and Nothingness* as a limit to my freedom, and, while the coefficient of adversity of things was revealed *only* through subjectivity, it was nevertheless *revealed*. Granted, that in *Being and Nothingness* Sartre emphasized the notion of freedom more than that of the situation in which freedom was always found, but it is quite another thing to say that he faced no other necessity than choosing himself. It may be that Orestes in Sartre's *The Flies* could not have been a Marxist, but Orestes is by no means the *only* embodiment of human freedom. In Sartre's *Dirty Hands*, the Communist functionary, Hoederer, is also portrayed as a freedom in search of its own destiny.

4

That Sartre's existentialism begins and ends with an "intuited personal freedom" seems equally dubious when the statement of his stance tends to assimilate it to the Stoic version of freedom upon which Sartre has consistently cast scorn. The notion that a man is fully free as long as he may think even if not speak what he wishes is one which Sartre finds ludicrous. If it were plausible to read *Being and Nothingness* in this fashion, Sartre would be obliged by his own principles to write another book in which freedom was shown in its embodiment, shown in its alienation, and shown in its advance to its further self. If a Stoic freedom were lost in the process, that is as it should be— *from Sartre's point of view.* It is even possible to argue that the standpoint of *Being and Nothingness* would indeed have been abandoned if Sartre had not written a book in which freedom was put in peril to such an extent that some would hold that it had been abandoned. No one has more clearly linked knowledge and action than has this man and no one has said more clearly that every finality produces a counter-finality. We do not attempt to spell out this interpretation here, but to suggest its outlines is to indicate a more plausible interpretation of the move from *Being and Nothingness* to the *Critique* than the one called abandonment—at least *if one takes Sartre's point of view.*

We contend that Warnock's assertion concerning the transition in Sartre's thought is a result of the kind of "exaggeration" of which both she and Anthony Manser accuse Sartre, an exaggeration which stems from underplaying freedom's bonds and overplaying the literary conception of radical freedom. Another view must be taken of Warnock's assessment of Sartre's Marxism. Here the problem is not so much exaggeration as it is a failure to distinguish the variety of Marxism which Sartre endorses from what he calls the "Stalinist" or "idealist" versions of Marxism, versions which he has explicitly repudiated. An unequivocal and readily available statement of his position on these matters is contained in a long footnote which occurs in what became the preface to the *Critique*, the portion translated under the title, *Search for a Method*.[3] In that note, Sartre gives a criticism of "idealist" Marxism by impugning this view which lays claim to objectivity and thus amounts to the assumption of nonsituated observation. He says that such observation is impossible after knowing but a moment of a totalizing action, that the "only theory of knowledge which can be valid today is one which is founded upon the truth of microphysics: the experimenter is a part of the experimental system." Such a theory of knowledge must "situate knowing in the world." It would show that the act of reflection through which we first become aware of the situation would not initiate the action, but would be produced by the process as its own clarification without obscuring the fact that the act was merely a moment of the totalizing action:

The truth is that subjectivity is neither everything nor nothing; it represents a moment in the objective process (that in which externality is internalized), and this moment is perpetually eliminated only to be perpetually reborn. Now, each of these ephemeral moments—which rise up in the course of human history and which are never either the first or the last—is lived as a *point of departure* by the subject of history. "Class consciousness" is not the simple lived contradiction which objectively characterizes the class considered; it is that contradiction already surpassed by *praxis* and thereby preserved and denied all at once. But it is precisely this revealing negativity, this distance within immediate proximity, which simultaneously constitutes what existentialism calls "consciousness of the object" and "nonthetic self-consciousness."[4]

Sartre clearly supposes that there exists a foundation in his technical philosophy for his efforts in *Critique de la Raison Dialectique*.[5] Even a Marxist who was sympathetic to Sartre's reservations about orthodox Marxism could grant that there was such a foundation, indeed, he might well be disturbed by what some unsympathetic Marxists have called Sartre's "voluntarist" tendencies. He might even endorse an autocritique. What would happen, for instance, if one asked whether or not

6

the claim Sartre makes applies to itself? Presumably it is a piece of knowledge. If that is so, then the epistemology recommended above would have to be applied to itself, for the theory presented is apparently intended to be perfectly general. From what situation, then, does it spring? It would appear that Sartre's first principle of epistemology cannot account for itself. One might try to avoid this charge in a number of ways. For instance, one might hold that the language in which Sartre's assertion is couched is misleading and that this piece of knowledge is to be exempted from the restrictions placed upon all other such statements. That the claim might be considered in this light is suggested by the fact that earlier, in *Search for a Method*, Sartre speaks of Marxism as a general perspective within which facts are studied so as to enrich our understanding and to clarify action. The statement that there is no nonsituated knowing may well be merely a linguistic expression of just such a general orientation. At a time when so much of the work done by philosophers of various persuasions is programmatic, it is tempting to construe a general perspective, or, rather, the linguistic expression of such an orientation, as a heuristic principle or even a stipulation. Either way it would not be a claim and, being thus neither true nor false, would not count as knowledge. Thus it might avoid being "situated."

What we mean to show is that while Sartre's epistemological stance is open to dialectical assault, it is not without weapons with which to be defended. But we learn more if we take Sartre at his word and examine what is revealed of the Marxism to which he is opposed by the character of the assault upon him. Sartre's contention is that knowledge is always situated in the world. One is immediately reminded of Lenin's claim that consciousness is only the reflection of being, or of the contemporary Marxist claim that one's philosophical position merely reflects his class standing. Either reading should be acceptable to an orthodox Marxist but neither would be acceptable to Sar-

7

tre. If the contemporary Marxist interpretation were taken, it would immediately be seen to be self-frustrating. That opinion could only be a reflection of the class standing of its proponents. But those who endorse such a stance do assert and must assert that there is a plurality of classes and therefore a plurality of reflections which are their respective philosophies. If an orthodox Marxist asserts that these classes are mutually exclusive, their respective philosophic reflections must also be mutually exclusive. Thus, to argue against another system is simply to shout that "He's wrong *because* I'm right," and while that is good fun it is scarcely effective polemic. The other position can only be impugned internally. But a precondition for internal attack is a thorough comprehension of the opposing position. How shall an orthodox Marxist achieve that comprehension? His knowledge of that position will presumably share the characteristic of all of his knowledge, that of being a reflection of his own class standing. All he can attack is *his* version of the errant system. No claim is made that this difficulty is peculiar to Marxism. To discern exactly what a philosopher says or means is a task whose difficulty is legendary and very much with us today. But the difficulty is particularly acute for the orthodox Marxist, for not only does he have preconceptions—as who doesn't—but he *must* have them, and he cannot surpass them until the material conditions of life have changed so that he may surpass them. As Sartre points out when speaking of George Lukacs' failure to understand Heidegger or Sartre, even given Lukacs' position as an intelligent Marxist theoretician:

Yes, Lukacs has the instruments to understand Heidegger, but he will not understand him; for Lukacs would have to *read* him, to grasp the meaning of the sentences one by one. And there is no longer any Marxist, to my knowledge, who is still capable of this. . . . This is because they insist on standing in their own light. They reject the hostile sentence (out of fear or hate or laziness) at the very moment that they

8

want to open themselves to it. This contradiction blocks them. They literally do not understand a word of what they read.[6]

To use Kantian language, the Marxist always deals with the phenomenal Other but instead of dealing with him through categories constitutive of any consciousness, he deals with the Other through categories of what *he* grants is a particular class consciousness. That is phenomenal!

None of this orthodox Marxist set is acceptable to Sartre. Insofar as they are self-admitted proponents of a class view, particularity which is unsurpassable restricts their comprehension. Where they speak of the proletariat as the universal class, and of its ideology as "objective," they take the standpoint of the Absolute, of the universal consciousness. But any flirtation with notions of universal and particular consciousnesses, Sartre holds, leads straight to idealism, the ideology of the bourgeoisie:

> The game is played on two levels; there is in Marxism a constituting consciousness which asserts *a priori* the rationality of the world (and which, consequently, falls into idealism); this constituting consciousness determines the constituted consciousness of particular men as a simple reflection (which ends up in a skeptical idealism). Both of these conceptions amount to breaking man's real relation to history.[7]

In the face of such unequivocal comment, to treat Sartre's views as one might be tempted to treat orthodox Marxist views would be ludicrous. How, then, shall we understand Sartre's advocacy of "situated" knowledge? Two of his remarks seem immediately relevant to this question. First, he criticizes contemporary Marxists, Lukacs, for example, for their version of situating. He complains that they attempt to treat concrete human beings or synthetic totalities by exhibiting them as mere instances of the most general principles of Marxism. To do this is to make them into object-men in a world of objects. Sartre insists that these most general principles be used in conjunction with "mediations" which will take cognizance of such things

9

as concrete men involved in their actions, their basic conditioning, their family background, the ideological instruments they utilize, and the particular environment of their actions. Second, Sartre speaks of a time when we shall not find ourselves in the "situation" which is now ours, in particular, we shall not find class position as fundamental a determinant as it has been, for as soon as ". . . there will exist *for everyone* a margin of real freedom beyond the production of life, Marxism will have lived out its span; a philosophy of freedom will take its place."[8] From within *this* situation, which makes Marxism the philosophy within which all other apparent philosophies are mere ideologies, Sartre speaks of a time when Marxism will be surpassed.

That we can speak in this manner is scarcely surprising if we take Sartre's own statement of his position seriously:

A flight and a leap ahead, at once a refusal and a realisation, the project retains and unveils the surpassed reality which is refused by the very moment which surpasses it. Thus knowing is but a moment of *praxis*, even its most fundamental one; but this knowing does not partake of an absolute knowledge. Defined by the negation of the refused reality in the name of the reality to be produced, it remains the captive of the action which it clarifies, and disappears along with it.[9]

Sartre's human reality is not "in" a situation in the sense in which some Marxists hold that an individual is "in" a class. To be "in," the human reality must also be beyond. To speak of a situation of which Marxism is the dominant philosophy, the human reality would have to be able to speak of a time when that situation—and thus Marxism—would be no more. Sartre insists that we must speak in this manner. The future does influence the present since it is ingredient in it. Man is his possibilities although one can speak of those only in outline based upon the actual structures of the here and now. To suppose that the human reality might be simply a function or reflection of his present circumstances betrays a fundamental misunderstand-

10

ing of Sartre's doctrine. No doubt he has many puzzles involved in his formulation but this is not one of them.

It is the ready availability of such counter-evidence which is the chief source of our astonishment at claims like Warnock's. Even this brief sketch of the differences between his version of Marxism and the orthodox type is enough to indicate that his version is far from the usual account and thus is not obviously inconsistent with his radical view of freedom. Yet Sartre has called himself Marxist and he has acknowledged that he had to go to school to Merleau-Ponty in order to increase his awareness of the weight of man's social being to the point where he could write *CRD*. It is also true that, with the exception of a rather casual assessment of Sartre's variety of Marxism, his detractor's account does not rest so much upon false evidence as it does upon the failure to attend closely to the philosophic core of Sartre's later views, the notion of dialectical reason. Our task, then, is to show that there is another reading of his early period which is more plausible than that which his critics favor and then to show that a concentration upon the essential themes of *CRD* will support our contention that there is greater continuity than discontinuity in Sartre's thought. It is to that task that we now turn.

One

FREEDOM

AND

SITUATION

Although Sartre had produced no small amount of both literary and philosophical work by the closing years of World War
II, we begin our account of his early period with the efforts
which cluster around his "phenomenological ontology," *Being
and Nothingness*.[1] The book was massive—six hundred pages
—frequently ill written, and filled with an intriguing mixture
of brilliant insights and some of the most torturous philosophical reasoning seen since Hegel. Incredible patience and considerable training were necessary to deal with it seriously and
thus it was available only to a limited audience. No doubt many
of the objections offered to *Being and Nothingness* can be
traced to the lack of one or both of these capacities so that
Sartre might well have disdained such carping. But, because
his commitment to living his world through the word has always been more fundamental to him than a particular mode of
communication, Sartre chose to respond to some of these objections in their own terms. Although it would be unfair to char-

acterize his literary activity merely as a device to exhibit his ideas in a "popular" form, his plays and novels certainly had that result. The same may be said of many of the essays which appeared in the journal which he and Merleau-Ponty edited, *Les Temps Modernes*. As an editor, Sartre had a guaranteed outlet for the dissemination of his ideas. Portions of his longer pieces have occurred in various issues of the journal. Other essays provided a vehicle through which Sartre was able to comment upon the issues of the day and to be involved in an important way in the debates which swirled through postwar France. Finally, he involved himself in various speaking engagements in which the question inevitably arose as to the relationship of his "philosophical" works to his contemporary commentary, and Sartre made little effort to avoid such questions.[2] In short, Sartre was then as he is now a man of letters who happened also to be a very competent philosopher.

It would be interesting to know whether some of the Anglo-Saxon response to Sartre's thought was dependent upon the relative availability of his plays and short essays as contrasted to the relative inaccessibility of *Being and Nothingness* and *Les Temps Modernes*. Were this assessment plausible, one could understand why many who knew Sartre through translation formed a view of his opinions which they now say he has betrayed. Certainly the plays, the novels, and the essay, "Existentialism is a Humanism," depict the familiar lonely, anguished, fiercely free individual who has been spoken to at such great length by thinkers from Kierkegaard to Heidegger and beyond. These writings are not limited to this theme, but there is no question that it stands out from them. When *Being and Nothingness* became available in English, the theme was reinforced. Many have said correctly that there is no other systematic work which represents so radical a portrait of human freedom. But in the other pieces which Sartre published in *Les Temps Modernes*, particularly "Materialism and Revolution,"

14

this man who took himself as the model for his conception of the human reality revealed himself, if not as a Marxist, certainly as a member of the "noncommunist Left" and often as an active Communist sympathizer.[3]

One suspects that not only did some Anglo-Saxons lack acquaintance with the full breadth of Sartre's work but they also lacked either the information or the ideological distance to understand how this apostle of freedom could suppose that a commitment to Marxism or to Communism could be a commitment made in the name of freedom. Sartre's commitment was made during and after the second World War, during the same period of time which presumably gave rise to the attitudes of some of his readers which produced their puzzlement. Sartre has said that his commitment to Communist causes did not become fixed until 1950 but his preference for "leftist" opinions has its roots in his experience of the war. The defeat of Facism gave great encouragement to those who hoped for the Revolution because they believed that the conquest of France and the misadventures of the Vichy regime had so discredited and undermined the power structure as to make its resurgence impossible. They firmly believed that there would, of necessity, be something different and possibly something better. That the Communists would hold a place of power in the new society seemed beyond doubt. Whatever ideological differences had separated the left intellectuals from the Communist party before the war had become irrelevant in the face of cooperation during the Occupation. The disciplined militancy of the Communists had made them the nucleus of the Resistance, the most effective of the *maquis*. Men had seen the fact of the subordination of factional interest to the greater good. The militancy of the Communists was a large part of the reason for their effectiveness and, in the context of the joint struggle against the national and ideological enemy, that intransigence had become a positive virtue instead of the barrier to coopera-

15

tive effort which it had been in prewar days. This new cooperation continued after the war during the period of the Popular
Fronts. Sartre tells us that some of the young men who had
committed themselves to the Party were disturbed because it
did cooperate instead of seeking to institute the Revolution.
This honeymoon was not to last long, but at that time only the
cadre knew that the policy of the Party was merely a temporary
response to external circumstances, to the necessity of rebuild-
ing the citadel of Socialism, Russia, in the face of the possession
of atomic weapons by the capitalist West.

Whether Sartre was one of those who knew this at the time
is not clear, but his understanding of Communism as a massive
action in the name of freedom must be considered in the light
of these circumstances. This petty bourgeois *littérateur* was
deeply impressed by the effectiveness the Communists had displayed as well as by the self-sacrifice of the militants. Above all,
they were men of action. Sartre's writing, particularly "What
is Literature," reveals his ancient concern that the writer's trade
was but a pale imitation of "real" commitment. One senses too
much protest in his repeated affirmations to the contrary and
his abortive venture in helping to form the political party, the
Rassemblement du Peuple Francais, may be partly attributed to
this recurrent fear of impotence. That venture was also due to
Sartre's growing realization that the left coalition was beginning to fall apart. The *ancien régime* was beginning to con-
solidate its return to grace and to resume its former position of
power. DeGaulle had come to the fore to be succeeded by a be-
wildering succession of petty politicians representing various
fragments of the old masters. The failure of the *RPF* was but
one of many symptoms of the demise of revolutionary aspiration. In the midst of an ambiguity which was moving inexor-
ably toward the prewar arrangement with the Right in power
and the Left in protest, the stubborn intransigence of the Communists was a hard, clear light. The Communists were clearly

16

mistaken on some major issues of doctrine and of tactics, but at least one could tell where they were mistaken. One could begin to make a case for the claim that their mistakes were excesses, consequences of the determinateness of their doctrine and, given the virtues of definiteness, such excesses might well be indulged or tolerated. That they might be so indulged was also due to the fact that, negatively, they were consistently on the right side, that is, against the oppressors. One finds again and again in Sartre intimations of the vow he was later to swear against the bourgeoisie. The capitalist pigs were clearly the enemy of man, and enmity toward them was always a sign of good faith, even if of confused good faith. The Communists, in short, were revolutionaries, men who appreciated the tenacity of the social malignancy which was the Right and who advocated the radical surgery which was required for its removal. The resurgence of the Right had shown clearly that nothing short of extermination would suffice. Sartre became convinced that capitalism was a social and political order which *systematically* kept the greater part of mankind in a near sub-human status and thus was wholly inconsistent with the ideology of freedom it professed. Until it was overthrown, *men* would not be fully free, and thus *man* would not be fully his freedom.

It was against this background and in the context of these opinions that Sartre published the works through which he achieved his status with the general literate public as the advocate of the most radical conception of freedom among us. But the setting of these efforts is easily forgotten if one concentrates upon the bulk of his dramatic output or upon the most famous of his popular essays, "Existentialism is a Humanism." Sartre makes his case so strongly and so persuasively that, not only is it easy to suppose that this essay is an accurate exposition of his position in *Being and Nothingness* and is thus canonical, but it is equally easy to suppose that his other activities were "personal" rather than "philosophical." The impact of "Exis-

17

tentialism is a Humanism" is due in part to the fact that it is written in the form of a defense. Playing the role of the beleaguered champion, Sartre situates his views in a context of controversy; defending himself, Sartre illuminates the opinions of his opponents by contrast to his own. The essay is an intellectual street brawl in which the champion makes his challengers look bad without showing deep concern for his own apparent inconsistencies. For all the drama attaching to a championship bout, it is what the smart money would call an unfortunate promotion. Yet, it *is* an occasion, and what one does find is a massive statement of the structure of human freedom in act with consequences rigorously drawn. The human reality is depicted as finding himself in a world in which there are no fixed or immutable guides. Neither values nor standards nor procedures wait to compel or lead him. This is not to say that the world into which he is thrown entirely lacks rule or law or order. Nature, itself, exhibits partial orders, indeed, resistance must be apparent or freedom will not have the contrast necessary to find itself and to find itself meaningful. Social reality also presents various levels of order—family, class, nation, and the rest. But Sartre holds that all such social arrangements are man made. Since Sartre's essay asserts and assumes that there is no God, divine fiat is not available as that to which one can appeal as the source of social order. Is invention by humans the only other alternative? Some have thought that, instead, we might appeal to a "natural" order, to values ingredient in the nature of things, where nature is understood to be uncreated. If man could be seen as having a "nature," an essence which he *could* not escape and *should* not try to escape, then we might speak of *necessary*, or at least of *desirable*, guides of conduct. Self-realization theories are no strangers to the history of philosophy nor are theories which postulate a "real" me or a "true self" which is somehow fugitive but capable, in principle, of being unearthed. But these anthropological analogues to the

18

reality-behind-the-appearances set of so much of traditional philosophy are no more acceptable to Sartre than is the set itself. "The first principle of existentialism is that man makes himself." Man finds himself in a world which he did not ask to enter, a world in which his proper name calls his attention to what he has come to be. With a body of various dimensions, attitudes of varying intensity, with tasks and sorrows and joys, he finds himself in a family with roles to play and a future to actualize. Reflection suggests to him that he has not always been thus, although some of the elements he notes seem to him to be enduring. He notices that in the events of the past which he parades before him, there seems to be a self which is not wholly different from the one who now reflects. He is both spectator and participant although in different modes. Is this the "real" self, the "true self"? If so, it is curiously without content. When he asks himself what it is or was, the various selves he constructs and the various relations he traces among them seem a curious combination of intimate and alien. What is more impressive, however, is that there are *various* selves and more than one way to reconstruct the route from the past to the present. Was he any of those selves? Yes, of course, But was he *only* those? It is a bit difficult to think of one's self as a plurality. Perhaps that is a partial motive for attempting to trace a route from earlier selves to later selves in such a way that the earlier selves are constituted as the ground of the later selves. One could at least hope to discover an ordered sequence which might be a "real" me. That would be comforting, for it would give flesh to the intimation that I, the reflector, am somehow one, somehow something. But the very availability of alternative routes mitigates against this hope. Where there are alternatives, to embrace any one of them is to choose rather than to be coerced. While one wants to say that what he has been was something in independence of the activity of recollection now performed, he cannot *now* say what it was. Some of the aspects

19

of past selves exhibit themselves as beyond present manipulation, but any totality we discern will be a mixture of these transient features and the deliverances of the vagaries and hesitations of memory, imagination, intellect, and current circumstances. If what I have been is part of "myself," clearly, I make myself.

But what can I say of that self which is now and that which will be? Surely one need not linger long to say that I shall make myself whatever I shall be. I will do so, of course, "on the basis of" what I have been and what I am. Whatever my current status may be, it both enhances and circumscribes the field of future possibilities. What-has-been is ambiguous in the grasp we have of it but even more ambiguous in its influence upon us. It is both enabling and restricting. If I can follow an intricate argument, it is in part because of years of practice in that activity. But the same discipline makes it difficult for me to deal with nonarguments or with arguments which exhibit the kind of sinuosity which does not yield to the skills and techniques I have internalized. If I will pay the penalty, I can even try to offset this double influence of academic discipline, perhaps through exercising my "native intelligence." The success of such efforts is not here in point. What is in point is that the actualization of this possibility is open to me. One may take the occurrence of the *attempt* with the same seriousness as Husserl took Descartes' attempt to doubt. That is enough to refuse the notion that myself-as-future must be a *function* of myself-as-past. There may well be characteristics which endure through all three temporal extases but not all of what I shall be consists of these, any more than all of what I have been consists of them.

My present self is a more difficult case, for here I think that I directly encounter that fugitive self who "reflects," although I encounter him in most intimate association with what he has been, will be, and, perhaps, is. I cannot avoid noticing that there is a distance between my past selves, or my future self, and me. I can, for instance, *consider* them but I *live* my present self. What I mean to do is to distinguish between the self that lives and the self that is lived while still insisting that what we have is what Sartre would call a "distance within immediate proximity." To say, however, that one self is "distinguished" from another is somewhat misleading, for, in asking about the aspects of the self which lives, we discover that we have simply enriched the self which is lived. The "reflecting" I is now fugitive. Could this be the "real" me for which I have sought? If so, the reason it could not be found is that it has that curiously empty character I attributed to the continuing I among the various selves which could be reconstructed. But this is the clue to the fact that I cannot have a fixed human nature. "What" I am, the "self" that I am, arises only on the occasion of reflection, and the reflecting I escapes in the process. That is not all. The self which is "left behind" is partly the result of the very reflections which liberated the fugitive I. Sartre puts the point more strongly: "If man as the existentialist sees him is not definable, it is because to begin with he is nothing."[4] The strength of the statement is worth noting. If our prior account faithfully reflects Sartre's view, the statement quoted from him is an overstatement. We wish to argue among other things that it is precisely this sort of overstatement which has misled some into supposing that a commitment to freedom forbade a commitment to embodied freedom.

That such statements on Sartre's part are overstatements can be further illustrated by attending to his habit of offering a claim at its full strength first and only later making modifications which he knows and we know are necessary. Part of his explication of the notion that man makes himself is as follows: "Man simply is. Not that he is simply what he conceives himself to be, but he is what he wills, and as he conceives himself after already existing—as he wills to be after that leap toward

21

existence. Man is nothing else but that which he makes of himself."[5] But how can these lines reflect the opinions of a man who has said again and again that the will is an abstract notion, not to be confused with the project, and, further, that conception is but a moment of praxis which turns back to clarify that praxis and is in no sense the necessary condition of human action? Sartre knows that he has gone too far:

> . . . man will only attain existence when he is what he purposes to be. Not, however, what he may wish to be. For what we usually understand by wishing or willing is a conscious decision taken—much more often than not—after we have made ourselves what we are. I may wish to join a party, to write a book or to marry—but in such a case what is usually called my will is probably a manifestation of a prior and more spontaneous decision.[6]

How one wishes he would have pursued this point! Instead, there follows the beginning of the curious switch to the semi-Kantian ethic of universalization which has dismayed so many of those who have come upon this essay for the first time. One wonders how much better Sartre would have been understood if those who would have been intrigued and puzzled by the lines quoted above had not gone on in a search for contextual clarification only to encounter Kant. The point will arise again and will be treated in due course but one wishes it had not occurred here.

What does occur is a further explication of the human situation through stating the consequences of Sartre's characterization of the human reality as thus far drawn. Man is that creature who is in anguish, abandoned, and in despair. Some have said that if man invents his own law there is no need to strive, there are no obligations to meet, no judgments to be made. The libertine is justified—let us rejoice. Sartre says no. The complement of the lack of coercion is the absence of that to which one can appeal for justification or for excuse. Man is responsible for his own actions, totally responsible, for he is judge,

22

jury, and defendant. In an alienated world where one's very meanings are stolen, where one's intentions are distorted by the instruments through which they find embodiment, surprise is a constant companion, disappointment a familiar emotion, and horror no stranger. Whatever results is mine. True, I can assemble the facts. I can appeal to others for corroboration of my inferences and for help in becoming aware of my rationalizations. I can total up the values and the disvalues and estimate the intensity of the various entries on the list, but between the list and its total, between premises and conclusion, there occurs a gap as wide as nothing. Even when I assemble the evidence it will not entail the decision. That requires a commitment. The result, Sartre says, is anguish.

Is what we have here merely another example of his well known penchant for exaggeration? It would appear that the same man who has advocated a literature of extreme situations, the man who tells us to test the alertness of another by asking in what extremity the other first discovered his freedom, has simply transported his passion for intensity and the *outre* to the realm of philosophy. Even a critic with Gabriel Marcel's forbearance has noted Sartre's tendency to give a magnificent description of a "scandalous" circumstance and then to extend the structures revealed there over a domain which contains cases which cannot be viewed as legitimate instances of such structures. For instance, Marcel praises Sartre's revealing description of a man whose sadness at a funeral is partly exhibition and partly self-persuasion. But Sartre then uses this example as a model from which he leaps to the claim that we always afflict ourselves with sadness, that we never are sad as an inkwell is an inkwell, but always make ourselves to be sad. Have we just another instance of Sartre's tendency to over-hasty generalization? Even if we tentatively accept the rather summary dismissal of deity which is given in the course of Sartre's discussion of abandonment, surely we are not wholly

23

alone. When we are ill, we do not hesitate to seek medical aid. Lawyers, clergy, teachers, scientists, all these and more stand ready to aid us when our need is great and our inquiry sincere. Sartre will have none of this. It is common human experience that experts disagree. We are thrown back upon our own decision as to which expert we shall endorse. But, even more fundamentally, one must ask what it is to be an authority. Sartre says it is to be *chosen* to be one. To go to another for advice is to confer that status upon him. If we commit ourselves in advance to accepting his instruction, it is clear that he has been invested with authority by virtue of that commitment. If one has what one thinks may be an encounter with the divine and one goes to a psychiatrist for consultation, the chips are already down. But even if one seeks advice with the proviso that it may be accepted or rejected, the proviso represents the fact that not only does one choose, but one *must* choose.

The account above seems to neglect the fact, that many choose the same man as an authority, which suggests that those who attain the status of an authority do not attain it in quite the idiosyncratic manner indicated. Even if it were true that there is no appeal beyond commitment, even if multiple commitments were simply additive, one may, nevertheless, draw sustenance from the actions of one's fellows. The strength which emerges from solidarity is a favorite theme of Sartre himself, and, whatever may be the intricacies of his own version of Marxism, whoever calls himself Marxist must respect the values of class consciousness and class action. Sartre tells us that his vacillation on this point has been the object of some of the most fierce assault he has suffered from his leftist brethren. They have held that one who tells us, as Sartre does, that he is committed to man can scarcely treat our common humanity as lightly as this neglect of consensus indicates. Sartre's response to such objections is unequivocal. Unlike the orthodox Marxists, Sartre does not hold that the reality in which we find ourselves exhibits a necessary pattern, an inevitable process, which, by exhibiting itself in the behavior of men, would allow us to count upon them without reservation. We find ourselves, instead, in a world of risk, in a world in which discontinuity is, in part, the result of the existence of a plurality of subjectivities. If I choose to commit myself to some joint venture, I may place my confidence in those committed to it, but to use that confidence as a justification for itself is to seek to act, not only where there is hope, but indeed where there is certainty of achievement, even if I shall have to be sacrificed to that eventual goal. We do not have such a refuge. We can, and we must, "act without hope." If we find comfort in the discovery that others *happen* to be embarked upon the same journey, that is all well and good. Such a fellow feeling may be a necessary condition for effective political action, and therefore we should engage in propaganda on its behalf. But that is quite different from saying that we who make propaganda must be its dupe, or at least its unwitting dupe. To accept a political creed, to accept a political leader, is not structurally different from accepting a religious creed or a divine guide. There are political movements and their leaders, but they cannot make themselves mine. I must choose them. Were there a God the case would not be different, for the clarion call of the prophet and the stern injunctions of the priest both suppose that I am capable of falling away from grace, precisely because I have fallen. There are authorities, there are standards, there may or may not be divine legislation, but none of them compel me unless I choose them. Man is condemned to be free.

What I shall be is what I make myself to be whether I like that or not. It is Sartre who has said that what the revolutionary demands is the ability to invent his own society, and the human condition described to this point certainly provides that opportunity. The goals a man pursues are those which he makes to be goals by that very pursuit. If that is so, it is hard to see how he might evaluate his chosen end. To evaluate it by some standard other than itself could only be to have opted for another such created value, and the same question would arise again. One might take that which one chooses and use it as a standard against which one judges other goals. But for Sartre there is, in principle, no standard which could be used to discriminate among alternative values. There are also practical problems. Once having made a commitment, one can judge other activities, attitudes, or projects as means relative to the chosen end or as factors which inhibit the achievement of that end. But, if the world in which we find ourselves is as risky as Sartre's discussion of despair suggests, judgments as events in that world must also exhibit that character of risk. If we consider assessment as the attempt to ascertain how well a particular action or attitude "fits" a more general standard, the third element in this activity, the *act* of judgment itself, must also partake of the uncertainty, the contingency, of the world. The depth of that contingency is most vividly exhibited in the claim that in an alienated world the fruits of our labor are necessarily stolen from us. Our intentions are objectified, externalized in forms where they are scarcely recognizable or in which they even become counterfinalities. Nothing is finally attained, nothing emerges in its pristine innocence. It is no more the case that anything can be wholly achieved than it is that there is anything upon which we can ultimately depend. There are some who would respond to this kind of world by withdrawing from all engagement. If the world is indifferent or is downright hostile to human efforts, a laggard would be even more inclined to abstain. As one of my friends in basic training once asked after hearing a lecture on the horrors of battle designed to firm his will in advance, "Where do I go to surrender, sir?"

One can sympathize with quietism as a response to Sartre's characterization of the human predicament, but that old fashioned moralist remains unmoved. Quietism is a possible re-

26

sponse, but it is neither necessary nor desirable in his eyes. On the other hand, Sartre cannot be surprised at this reaction, for it is he who has said that man is the useless passion to be whole, to be God, thus one would be foolish to expect any other response to him from the "all or nothing" crowd. But to say that man cannot be what he is and still be content with less than complete achievement is not to say either that this desire must be fulfilled or that the necessary failure to satisfy the desire eliminates all value in lesser achievement. Few philosophers today would endorse the belief that it is possible to give a complete, general account of the real in the form of a deductive system. As the realization has come upon us that there is a plurality of equally coherent formal systems in which we can arrange the same material, the passion for one system has dimmed. But one need not draw from this belief the conclusion that systematization itself must be without value. True, many contemporary philosophers hold this opinion, but, however understandable it may be as an historical response, it is not necessary. It is still possible to hold that one discovers elements through systematic arrangement which one is unlikely to discover by any other means A writer is repeatedly reminded that his audience can always draw consequences from what he has said which simply never occurred to him. Systematic arrangement can serve as a philosopher's own attempt to draw those consequences although he cannot, and should not, intend system as a means to prevent critical appraisal. Certainly Sartre has availed himself of this device although one cannot say that he has done so for these reasons. It is well known that one of Merleau-Ponty's fundamental objections to Sartre's work was precisely this fondness for system. The issue is complex, but this is enough to show that it is not *necessary* to suppose that, because the whole cannot be attained, no lesser achievement is possible or desirable. Sartre holds that limited success is both possible and desirable. His is a philosophy of activism, disillu-

27

sioned, perhaps, but no less impassioned because illusion has fled.

One can, for example, try to act so as to make freedom its own end. Sartre tells us that it is possible to make "moral judgments" to the effect that some action or attitude contributes to or detracts from, the incarnation of freedom. One might suppose that he is contending that men *should* seek to make freedom its own end. If that reading is acceptable, the radical character of his stance on choice is much less than has thus far been supposed. That men *can* act so as to objectify the freedom which they are, is beyond doubt, but clearly they *need* not do so and often have not done so. Whence, then, comes the ought? Men must act—granted. Even inaction has its consequence, chiefly, the maintenance of the status quo. But what can be meant by saying that they *should* act in some fashion rather than in another? Sartre implies that there is something incoherent about being a freedom and not acting to further it. This is perilously close to the recommendation that one be what one is, a recommendation of sincerity not open to Sartre after his treatment of that attitude in *Being and Nothingness*. It is precisely because one is free that one can act to objectify that freedom, but to act against it also presupposes freedom. Otherwise, freedom is not inescapable and man is not condemned to be free. One could understand that Sartre has freely chosen the objectification of freedom and, on the basis of that choice, urges its advancement. In this case it may be a good *tactic* to present the invitation to join him in the form of an imperative. Sartre is certainly no stranger to tactics. But one cannot deny that Sartre may himself be a victim of his own hypnotic spell.

Let us examine this possibility. The evidence in its favor consists chiefly of two earlier claims; first, the claim that in discovering oneself one discovers the Other, and, second, the peculiar, almost Kantian claim, which we mentioned earlier, that one should act as though the eyes of all men are upon us. Very little

28

is said about the first of these so that, beyond noting its occurrence, we must wait until our consideration, in the next chapter, of the lengthier analyses in *Being and Nothingness*. Here we shall simply quote Sartre's passing remark in "Existentialism is a Humanism" and then comment briefly:

Contrary to the philosophy of Descartes, contrary to that of Kant, when we say "I think" we are attaining to ourselves in the presence of the other, and we are just as certain of the other as we are of ourselves. Thus the man who discovers himself directly in the *cogito* also discovers all the others, and discovers them as the condition of his own existence. . . . Under these conditions, the intimate discovery of myself is at the same time the revelation of the other as a freedom which confronts mine, and which cannot think or will without doing so either for or against me. Thus, at once, we find ourselves in a world which is, let us say, that of "Inter-subjectivity." It is in this world that man has to decide what he is and what others are.[7]

It is by no means clear how one discovers the other in the *cogito*, nor does Sartre pursue the point so as to enlighten us. The theme itself is not new to Sartre's thought, since one of the warrants he offers for his assertion that the ego is transcendent is that only on that conception can solipsism be avoided. One recalls, also, the famous passages in *Being and Nothingness* when the Other is discovered through shame. But how the Other is discovered, and discovered as a limitation through the *cogito*, is extremely puzzling. What we are tempted to say here is that Sartre is so convinced of the necessity to establish the existence of a plurality of necessarily interrelated subjectivities that he confuses two quite distinct issues. He is anxious to refuse the charge of subjectivism with which he has been confronted by critics as different as the Communists and Merleau-Ponty, since that subjectivism would forbid him anything but an aesthetic morality. At the same time, he wishes to emphasize that the general ontic structures to which he alludes are nothing unless they are "lived." Subjectivity in this sense is essential to his view, so essential that he will later charge ideal-

29

ist Marxists with so neglecting this feature of the social world that existentialism must continue in independence of the Marxism within which it should be a mere ideology. To make this sort of subjectivism seem plausible, Sartre invokes the *cogito* and then, in his zeal to keep this subjectivism nonsolipsistic, associates the *cogito* with a discovery of the Other through an intuition which is elusive at best.

Even more puzzling is his advocacy of what for all the world sounds like a variety of a Kantian position in moral philosophy. The claim is so strange that we will quote Sartre at considerable length lest we unwittingly misrepresent him:

When we say that man chooses himself, we do mean that every one of us must choose himself; but by that we also mean that in choosing for himself he chooses for all men. For in effect, of all the actions a man may take in order to create himself, as he wills to be, there is not one which is not creative, at the same time, of an image of man such as he believes he ought to be. To choose between this or that is at the same time to affirm the value of that which is chosen; for we are unable ever to choose the worse. What we choose is always the better; and nothing can be better for us unless it is better for all. . . . I am thus responsible for myself and for all men, and I am creating a certain image of man as I would have him to be. In fashioning myself I fashion man. . . . There is nothing to show that I am Abraham: nevertheless I also am obliged at every instant to perform actions which are examples. Everything happens to every man as though the whole human race had its eyes fixed upon what he is doing and regulated its conduct accordingly. So every man ought to say "Am I really a man who has the right to act in such a manner that humanity regulates itself by what I do?" If a man does not say that, he is dissembling his anguish.[8]

And even further, in the context of speaking of "moral judgments":

We will freedom for freedom's sake, in and through particular circumstances. And in thus willing freedom, we discover that it depends entirely upon the freedom of others and that the freedom of others depends upon our own. Obviously, freedom as the definition of a man does not depend upon others, but as soon as there is a commitment, I

30

am obliged to will the liberty of others at the same time as my own. I cannot make liberty my aim unless I make that of others equally my aim. Consequently, when I recognize, as entirely authentic, that man is a being whose existence precedes his essence, and that he is a free being who cannot, in any circumstances, but will his freedom, at the same time I realize that I cannot not will the freedom of others. . . . Thus although the content of morality is variable, a certain form of morality is universal. Kant declared that freedom is a will both to itself and to the freedom of others. Agreed: but he thinks that the formal and the universal suffice for the constitution of a morality. We think, on the contrary, that principles that are too abstract break down when we come to defining action. . . . The content is always concrete, and therefore unpredictable; it has always to be invented. The one thing which counts, is to know whether the invention is made in the name of freedom.[9]

There are few passages in the history of philosophy which are so snarled, so full of what are at least apparent inconsistencies, and to such an extent inconsistent with the essay in which they occur. To a sympathetic reader, they are infuriating. Were they not followed on frequent occasion by commentary which relieves their opaqueness, one would be tempted to reject Sartre out of hand. From what dim recesses of the philosophic tradition did Sartre dredge up, "What we choose is always the better; and nothing can be better for us unless it is better for all"? On what possible grounds can one who claims that men demand the right to invent their own law assert, "So every man ought to say, 'Am I really a man who has the right to act in such a manner that humanity regulates itself by what I do?'" A revolutionary, Sartre tells us elsewhere, is the man who denies the very notion of rights. How can that being which is in question in its being be "really" anything? If to act for freedom admits of the most diverse expressions, how does humanity *regulate itself* on the basis of some particular content? But, most fundamentally, how did the "ought" get in there in the first place? Nothing is an obligation for Sartre unless it is taken as such—and nothing need be taken.

The second quotation from Sartre's discussion of "moral

31

judgments" only deepens the difficulties, because it comes from the moral context. Sartre may well have a systematic right to talk of *logical* judgments, that is, of claims that some individual is offering reasons or engaging in actions which indicate that he is incapable of having done other than he has done. One can say that such claims are inconsistent with the constitution of the human reality if one accepts Sartre's description of that being as one which is what it is not and is not what it is. If one is committed to consistency, this might be understood as an evaluation, although Sartre does not explicitly characterize this judgment as anything other than descriptive. But how to get from this sort of judgment to a moral judgment which takes freedom as its own end and grades actions with respect to that standard is much less obvious. If we do this—and it is clear that for Sartre we do not always do so—how do we discover the mutual dependence of our freedom and that of the Other, that scandal which is perceived as a threat? "I cannot make liberty my aim unless I make that of the Other equally my aim." And how do I manage to assert that I cannot but will the freedom of others as soon as I recognize my own as that which I cannot but will?

Something has gone awry, but, before attempting to account for it, let us consider the modifications Sartre offers lest we carelessly distort his view. "To choose between this or that is at the same time to affirm the value of that which is chosen." If this line can be understood to mean that what is chosen *becomes* a value by virtue of the fact that it is chosen, then one can understand why "we are unable ever to choose the worse." If what the human reality will be is simply the ensemble of choices made by individual men, then we can understand "that in choosing for himself he chooses for all men." It is unfortunate that this point is put in a context which suggests that one holds before himself a vision of what man ought to be, a vision to which one attempts to make his actions conform or which his

32

actions are intended to realize. One wishes again that Sartre had developed the point, which he only mentions, that choice is not a matter of *willing* a consciously envisioned end but rather a matter of internalizing a "prior and more spontaneous decision." Instead, Sartre began his excursion into the Kantian routine. Were the point developed, the lines under consideration might well be understood in a much more plausible manner, for instance, that to act is to affirm the terminus of that act which, itself, will be an integral element of the ensemble called the "image of man." That we *do* create man through our choices may be argued from a Sartrean position. That we *ought* to have created what we have created, or that we *should* maintain that creation, is quite another point. Since we do create man, we may feel the need to remember that this is so, that, in part, the whole human race will be what it is because of what *this* human does. In Sartre's leftist mood, our intentions and their distorting externalizations have consequences whether these are envisioned or not. If this is merely an injunction to remember these things, all well and good. But, apart from the desire to make the Sartrean view consistent, the only point of access to this claim is the little phrase "as though" which may be supposed to indicate that pretense is required to entertain the continued gaze of the Other. That is a great deal to load upon one little phrase. If our anguish is so likely to be suppressed, if bad faith is the constant temptation to man that Sartre elsewhere insists it is, perhaps one can make out some justification for this pretense as a heuristic device, much as part of the Marxist apparatus is recommended by Sartre as a heuristic device. It is recommended here that his claims be viewed in this fashion for the sake of according to him the courtesy of being understood as an advocate of a coherent position. One must add, however, that Sartre's language is certainly an impediment to any such charitable course and a deterrent to the suggested procedure.

This charitable reading of Sartre's stance may be extended to the associated statement that my freedom and that of others are interdependent. The claim is startling in itself when one recalls that it is Sartre who has analyzed so much of the fabric of human relations in terms of conflict, frequently in terms of actions whose whole purpose is to subdue the subjectivities one encounters as so threatening that either seduction or aggression are required. He is also the man who can casually remark that we shall keep the bloodletting in a revolution to a minimum, because some of the bourgeoisie will be needed as technicians and managers. The third line in this quotation is of some help in unraveling this puzzle. Freedom as the "definition of man" does not depend upon others, but *as soon as there is a commitment* I am obliged to will the liberty of others at the same time as my own. Given a commitment *and* a commitment to consistency, one can say that he is obliged to accept whatever the consequences of the original commitment may be. Being is contingently necessary. But it cannot be my "original" freedom, that freedom which defines me, which is here the correlate of a commitment. I am condemned to be free. If a commitment to freedom *in general* is what is in question, then one can understand that the freedom of the Other is my obligation, but the notion of freedom in general is a bit sticky. Vagueness alone does not eliminate it from consideration since the unembodied freedom spoken of immediately thereafter in this quotation is so nonspecific as to be referred to as something in the "name" of which we invent. If it is also true that two contrary expressions may both exemplify the commitment to freedom, it will have to be sufficiently vague, sufficiently ambiguous, to admit of contrary articulations. Perhaps one should suppose that the apprehension of one's own unavoidable freedom is one of the "flashes," of which Merleau-Ponty speaks, which in Sartre's framework have the function of singularizing the universal and universalizing the singular, thus affording pur-

34

chase upon freedom in general. But to extend to freedom in general and thus to the freedom of others the characteristic of being unable not to be willed, as I cannot but will my own freedom, is a dubious move at best. Once again Sartre's choice of language is horrendous. Why must he speak of a freedom which I cannot but "will"? And to invoke the ghost of Kant in this place is almost unforgivable. A pudgy Sartre is not an obviously appropriate substitute for an emaciated Kant.

The difficulties for a sympathetic reader of this essay do not permit themselves to be wholly resolved by a direct appeal to the essay itself. However one twists and turns, the portrait of the lonely individual which struck such a sympathetic chord in those like Mary Warnock is contained in this work in a setting which is, to say the least, *apparently* incoherent. This failure to account for difficulties by internal means tempts one to appeal to factors external to the essay itself. One is tempted to say that the essay we have focused upon here simply and deliberately reflects the ambiguity of the world in which we find ourselves. Neither the world in which Sartre lives nor the creative accounts which he has given of it are infected with the kind of clarity which is so cherished by Anglo-Saxon philosophers. Alternatively, one might say that what we have here is a familiar case of the sort of sloppy presentation which is almost dictated by the demands of an audience to which a popular lecture is given. But, if one must have recourse to external factors, a more plausible procedure would be to suppose that Sartre is simply engaged in persuasion rather than in argumentation. If it is true that freedom is devoid of specific content, if every decision is ultimately unjustifiable, then one cannot argue for any particular course of action by treating it as a consequence, much less as a *necessary* consequence, of some more fundamental ground. But, if to choose is to make what is chosen to be a value, one can scarcely allow those who would detract from that value to suppose that "you pays your money and you takes your choice." If

35

one also gives them credit for understanding and endorsing an ontological sketch which admits of such a response, one may well shift to persuasion *precisely because* argument in its usual form is unavailable. One can talk in such a way as to allow others to suppose that freedom should be its own end without omitting qualifying phrases and clauses which provide escape hatches if the occurrence of persuasion is noted. *That* would be the sort of technique which would be effective when writing for a general audience. If one is also a political activist, the shift to persuasion *without notification of the shift* would scarcely be an unfamiliar technique. Sartre does tell us that at the point in time when this essay occurs he was not yet irrevocably committed to his permanent enmity toward the bourgeoisie, but, instead, was as yet only a student of the revolutionary views already mastered by his friend and colleague, Merleau-Ponty. But at least he was a proponent of revolutionary ideas, and, in the essay called "Materialism and Revolution," he advocates tactics which would by no means preclude the shift to persuasion. One could emphasize the influence of the stance taken in "Materialism and Revolution" to an even greater extent. One might assume that Sartre is at least as much a revolutionary as he is a phenomenologist, that the commitment to man which prevented him from enduring societies which spoke of human freedom while systematically enslaving most men weighed as heavily with him as his wish to refuse the various anthropologies which would make man merely a "reflection" of being.

We propose the following as an external "accounting" for the apparent inconsistencies in Sartre's early position. In his phenomenologist-existentialist mood, Sartre presents a portrait of the lonely individual, of a man who is his freedom, who has no ready-made values or standards to which he can ultimately appeal, neither God, nor "natural" law, nor self. This abandoned man lives his world in anguish and despair, bears the full responsibility for each of his actions and their consequences,

36

and has, at best, limited control over his creations. This man, who is not able to be the coincidence with himself of which he is the desire, is also faced with the necessity of creating himself from moment to moment. "Man is nothing else but that which he makes of himself. That is the first principle of existentialism." If we can discover a man's basic commitment, if we can discover the original choice of being which he is, we can account for and judge subsequent action. The commitment, itself, we cannot judge. Logical judgments are available, given the choice and the subsequent mode of behavior. If we accept Sartre's contention that the human being is that being whose being is in question in its very being, if we accept his portrait of the human reality as that which is incapable of self-coincidence, then we can also allow him a logical judgment with respect to the consistency of the original choice and the perpetual lack of being which man is. But the moral judgment he claims is not so easily accepted. The activity of a psychiatrist in helping one to discover the nature and sources of his difficulties is a task at which he is peculiarly competent. Recommendations which he offers for the avoidance or solution of those difficulties is quite another problem. A good therapist will recommend only as a means of helping his patient to come to his own resolution, but some therapists have been known to go far beyond that limit. It seems that the temptation to exceed the bounds of the therapeutic activity is built into the second part of that activity. Shall we say that the therapist is *also* a man? Let us say the same of Sartre.

Let us also say again that Sartre's major emphasis in this defense has been upon this man, this free being, as alone in the world, but add firmly that he is alone *among others*. We have noted the curious, poorly explicated claim that in discovering oneself, one discovers others. We have noted that the essay was written as a defense against criticism stemming from widely separated points in the political spectrum, as widely separated

37

as Catholics and Communists. *They* at least thought Sartre was very much an influence upon others, albeit an unacceptable influence. The Catholic apologist, Gabriel Marcel, coined the phrase, "café philosopher," to imply that Sartre was neither ultimately serious nor ultimately involved in his world, and Sartre has accepted that soubriquet.[10] But that is far from saying that either Sartre or man as Sartre conceives him is an island unto himself. To live one's world as one inhabits a café may not be to be "with" others as the theistic existentialists have it, but it is certainly not be a hermit, a role which Sartre has never cherished. In the essay, "What is Literature?" he had spoken at length of the importance of the writer's role in social and political matters. Many of his contributions to *Les Temps Modernes* were as worldly as our initial account indicated. None can deny that, as a person and as a professional writer, Sartre was, and is, very much a man of his age. But some, notably Merleau-Ponty, have denied that Sartre's philosophical efforts have been an adequate correlate to his existential involvements. We mention Merleau-Ponty because his demur occurred during Sartre's early period, long before the appearance of *CRD* led some Anglo-Saxons to charge Sartre with betrayal of his existentialism. The result is delightfully paradoxical. Both Merleau-Ponty and Sartre's Anglo-Saxon detractors agree that in the period dominated by *Being and Nothingness*, Sartre's conception of freedom was so radical that it prevented any effective account of man as a social being. Merleau-Ponty condemns Sartre for this exaggeration. Those like Warnock condemn him for abandoning his early stance for the sake of sociology. The combination of these objections is so peculiar that we really should not have called it paradoxical. It is a comedy of errors.

That this situation is comic is beyond question, but why a comedy of *errors*? One can respond most readily by focusing upon another of Sartre's "popular" essays, the one alluded to earlier called "Materialism and Revolution." This was written in 1945 in response to a request from a Polish journal for a report upon the state of philosophy in France. The date is important, for it shows that in those years, in Sartre's "early" period, he was very much concerned about the relation of the philosopher to his world. Most important, he explicitly claimed that an ontology like his was required to advance the cause of the Revolution, and even the Socialist revolution. The essay begins, for instance, with the announcement that the youth of France are presented with an unfair dilemma, with a choice between an idealism which was merely a political instrument of oppression and a materialism which represented the thinking of the workers but which had been so debased that no man of intellectual honesty could embrace it. The task which Sartre proposed to pursue was to reinterpret Marxism as something other than and better than a materialism, and thus restore it to its rightful place as the reflection and guide of the Revolution. To Communists, this was not only an attack upon sacred doctrine but also an intellectual equivalent to the "Third Force" doctrine, and their wrath was awesome. They were infuriated because the first half of the essay is devoted to a mode of attack upon orthodox Marxism which was just plain patronizing. It is written as though Sartre were a medieval master correcting errant seminarians concerning their misunderstandings of revelation. He devotes much space in the early portion of the essay to casual instruction in Hegel's notions. He *explains* the dialectic to Marxists! He repeats the familiar charge that so anxious are these mistaken Marxists to remove the doctrine of inherent rights in its usual association with subjectivity that they destroy subjectivity itself. Men become object-men in a world of objects. It is difficult to see how such beings could achieve consciousness at all, much less the class consciousness which is a necessary condition of the Socialist revolution. Similarly, it was hard to see how consciousness could be a "reflection of being," or how the wholly material could give rise to something as different from itself as ideas. To whomever reads this portion of Sartre's essay, the notion is inescapable that it is his intent to chastise the sinners rather than to criticize them.

The very grossness of Sartre's polemic suggests what the second half of the essay confirms, namely, that his intellectual commitment is less to refutation than to reconstruction. What he is anxious to do is to bring into being a philosophical instrument which will be the articulation and the guide of revolution. One may ask whether this is a "third force," as the Communists claim, or whether it is "true" Marxism. There has been no little speculation as to whether Sartre was advocating and advancing the Marxism of the young Marx, the Marx of 1844, against the serious modification of that doctrine which began with the collaboration with Engels and continued in the hands of Lenin and other Soviet theoreticians. There is much evidence even in this essay that this was part of Sartre's intent. He speaks frequently with severe reservations about Engel's influence upon Marx and Marxist doctrine, and his attitude toward Stalin and neo-Stalinists can be described as contemptuous. He displays the characteristic scholar's concern for what the founder *really* said, and the quotation of chapter and verse is not infrequent. But, despite all this, Sartre's interest in orthodoxy is clearly a secondary concern. His chief interest is to develop an intellectual instrument adequate to the needs of the revolution. If that instrument is "true" Marxism, all well and good, but it is not of the essence.

What are the lineaments of such a doctrine? Sartre gives us the criteria which he commits himself to meet:

In order to account for these various requirements, a revolutionary philosophy ought to set aside the materialistic myth and endeavour to show: (1) That man is unjustifiable, that his existence is contingent, in that neither he nor any Providence has produced it; (2) That, as a result of this, any collective order established by men can be transcended toward other orders; (3) That the system of values current in a society reflects the structure of that society and tends to preserve it; (4) That it can thus always be transcended toward other systems which are not yet clearly perceived since the society of which they are the expression does not yet exist—but which are adumbrated and are, in a word, invented by the very effort of the members of society to transcend it.[11]

It is precisely this transcendence which a revolutionary philosophy must explain. What the revolutionary wants is the possibility for man to invent his own law but the law which he encounters in his life-world seems anything but man-dependent. There is law, there is order, there are courts to interpret, and police to enforce. There are penalties for him who violates that law and privileges for him who moulds his actions to accord with it. Man finds himself in a world which reflects the fixed substratum of order established by God or by nature in which he has apparently been assigned a place with all of its attendant rights and duties. But, in Sartre's eyes, men who are workers, oppressed people, are more aware of the duties than the rights, so much so that it is only slightly misleading to say that the oppressed have only duties and no rights. Here, as elsewhere, Sartre presents a portrait of the worker as a man who is subhuman because he is regarded by his masters as subhuman. The most obvious trait of the laborer in an industrialized society is interchangeability. To middle class Americans, the portrait is a caricature. True, assembly line work is scarcely edifying. Little effort or intelligence is required to put two washers and two nuts on two bolts ninety-two times an hour, eight hours a day. True, the work is wearying and effort is required to do anything during the week other than eat, sleep and work—or so it appears to a student doing summer labor. But the regular employees give a very different appearance. They are not unhappy with the miniscule demands of their tasks, in fact, they fiercely resist any attempt to move them to another such task or to one of greater complexity. The long hours on the relentless line are full of banter, full of the joy of eluding the work rules, of achieving

41

the required output quickly so that there is a moment of way-wardness. Shop romances flourish. Lunch periods and breaks, as well as breakdowns, provide opportunity for conversation and diversion ranging from a quarrel over real or imagined management infringement upon the provisions of the contract to seven card stud. At the end of the day, powerful, often luxurious, cars pour out of parking lots which may cover an area as great as that covered by the plant itself. At the end of the trip is food, drink, golf, a date, a new lawn, all paid for by the labor of the day. The work is not enjoyable for these regulars but it is endurable; it is wearying but not exhausting, and the weariness all but disappears in the washroom. Then there is always the weekend and the vacation.

Sartre is not unaware of such considerations. He has even echoed the Marxist line which explains the relatively improved position of the worker in some capitalist states as the result of the availability of colonial people for the exploitation necessary to the maintenance of capitalism. He also entertains the view that the bourgeois managers have learned painfully that they must allow some rights to the worker precisely because only this move will allow them to maintain their own rights and privileges. But their claim that such rights and privileges are part of the immutable nature of things is the point which is the weakest link in the chain of oppression. From the worker's point of view, there are positions, there are places in an order, but on occasion he sees no reason why *he* should not hold that position rather than the present incumbent. The *position* at first seems justified but the *person* who holds it is less obviously sanctified. Resentment resulting from this attitude will often lead the worker to believe that the person does not deserve the position at all, that blind chance, economic opportunity, and no little favoritism are chiefly responsible for the chance coincidence of person and position. But what can you do? You can't fight city hall. A few, of course, will rebel, that is, will try to improve their lot by becoming foremen or by taking training programs in their spare time which will fit them for advancement. Others will try to improve their position in the system by becoming union members, shop stewards, or even union officers. But most will remain at what they are doing, for the number of desirable positions is severely restricted, and the attainment of those positions requires additional effort. Finally, many workers—one suspects most workers—will hold that the same factors of ill chance, injustice, and most of all, favoritism which led to the status they now hold will prevent them from escaping it. The most frequent result of such opinions is that the worker accepts his status, griping all the way, while enjoying the benefits it provides for him, both in daily routine and in the private sphere which his labor supports. He will become fiercely possessive of the rights which his position entails, guard them zealously, and attempt to increase them or extend them to cognate domains. I have seen an assembly line stopped for an hour because some member of the managerial force indicated that 94 pieces instead of 92 should be turned out in a given hour, and have seen violence erupt over whether the management should be obliged to provide soap dispensers rather than bar soap in the washroom. With or without sufficient warrant, many workers feel that their rights can be maintained only through constant vigilance and sometimes only through steady increase. They feel themselves to be under constant threat from an Other whose actions display both the vigilance and the tendency to aggrandizement which the worker detects in himself. The depth of such feelings is indicated by the importance which such intrinsically trivial matters as those discussed above can assume. Only a deep-seated attitude could transform such transient issues into potential sources of violence and discord.

The worker's awareness that his rights are maintained only through constant effort on his part can suggest to him that this is the nature of rights in general, not merely of those which he happens to possess. His perspective involves the belief that the rights of his superiors are built into the position and the person who holds it acquires them only by assuming that position. The "brass," which rules, supports, and threatens him, consists of human beings like himself who are unjustifiable but who through contingency have been certified as the masters. Sartre tells us that the revolutionary must first dispense with the very notion of rights where rights are considered as an inherent characteristic of some humans. "We, too, are men." The very contingency which infects the world of the worker must be seen to extend to the manager. True, the worker zealously guards his own rights, but that very fervor expresses his awareness that his rights are by no means inherent, much less inalienable. They are exactly what he makes them and maintains them to be. A man who stuffs insulation into refrigerators has first call upon the air hose because he is the insulation man. If he is sufficiently courageous, he may be able to maintain that privilege even against a bigger man who attempts to have first crack at the hose by threatening physical violence. Both rights and privileges are attendant upon the position, and the position is exactly what he makes it to be. A possible extrapolation is obvious. The position held by the master with his rights and privileges must also depend upon the continued activities of human beings, the same unjustifiable human beings who are members of the species to which the worker belongs. The required response is transparent. If it is *this* system maintained by *these* human beings which oppresses him, let us destroy *this* system. ". . . revolution takes place when a change in institutions is accompanied by a profound modification in the property system." The system maintains and is maintained by those who profit from it. It was invented neither by some distant deity, nor by the laws of nature, nor by some of the immutable laws which the worker is told govern economic processes. The system was begun and is maintained by *men*, and thus it may be altered by men. Those who profit from it, of course, will fight to maintain it. Because they will, it is not only revolution which is required but violent revolution. But nothing less than revolution will do, for, if the men are destroyed and the system left intact, other men, perhaps even some of one's fellows, will simply become new masters. To destroy the system is to destroy those men, so one cannot speak of destroying the system and leaving the men intact. Since the system and those who exploit it are mutually supporting, the entire system must be demolished. Revolution must be done.

How is it possible for notions like these to occur to the worker? How is a person described as follows able to achieve the sort of consciousness required to conceive of revolution?

The situation of the revolutionary is such that he cannot share in these privileges in any way whatever. The only way that he can get what he wants is by the destruction of the class that oppresses him. This means that the oppression is not, like that of the Jews or the American Negroes, a secondary and, as it were, lateral characteristic of the social regime under consideration, but that it is, on the contrary, a constituent one. The revolutionary is, thus, both an oppressed person and the keystone of the society which oppresses him. In other words, it is as an oppressed person that he is indispensable to this society. That is, the revolutionary belongs to those who *work* for the dominant class.[12]

Such a situation, the situation within which the revolutionary thinks, cannot give rise to class consciousness on the account of it given by idealistic Marxists. An object-man in an object world is incapable of possessing the capability of transcendence which any conception of revolutionary thinking must endorse. What revolutionaries require, instead, is a philosophical theory which shows that action both reveals and modifies reality.[13] The revolutionary as laborer will discover his capacity for transcendence through *work*. Bound by the master to a restricted task, reduced nearly to the status of a thing, his work imposed upon him, and its end product stolen from him, the worker nevertheless discovers that he is the master of the infin-

45

itesimal range of physical things which surround him. *Because* those things are subject to universal laws, he is able to exploit them in his fashion. *Because* the master gives him a task which is so readily accomplished, he discovers his liberation from these things. One is tempted to read one of the classical elements of a dialectical movement into this. The project of the master, the Taylorist, is to maximize his gain by carrying the process of objectifying the worker to its extreme, but his success is so great that the activity gives rise to its opposite.

No claim is made that the worker's grasp of this circumstance is cognitive:

A worker is not a determinist in the way the scientist is; he does not make of determinism an explicitly formulated postulation. He lives it in his gestures, in the movement of the arm striking a rivet or pounding a crowbar. He is so thoroughly permeated with it that when the desired effect is not produced he tries to find out what hidden cause has prevented its realization, never conceiving of any waywardness or sudden and accidental break in the natural order. And since it is deep within his slavery, at the very moment at which the master's sweet pleasure transforms him into a thing, that action, by bestowing upon him sovereignty over objects and a specialist's autonomy over which the master has no power, liberates him, the idea of liberation is linked in his mind with that of determinism.[14]

"Linked" is almost too weak a term here, for, to the extent that the revolutionary can regard himself as a determined thing and can see that the masters, too, are men, he can divest them of their rights and associated privileges. Thus he may be tempted to accept the materialist myth, that explanation from below which would insist that the worker was a thing, rather than that which masters things. Sartre tells us that it is both the glory and the shame of materialism that it has served the worker as an instrument for liberation and a temptation to degradation, a temptation which provides a total determinism, an historical necessity before which history is a document to be deciphered rather than a task to be performed.[15]

46

But the worker is the man who knows better than most that the real is no dream, that it is apprehended through precisely that adversity which is the daily lot of the oppressed. He knows that mere thought will not prevail, that even after arduous labor ". . . there remains an unassimilable residue, the otherness, the irrationality, the opaqueness of the real. . ."[16] This lived resistance, however, is also the occasion for the discovery of transcendence. Although the worker is forced to engage in repetitive activity, through that very activity he notices the order and he notices that it could be ordered differently, hence, the strict injunctions laid upon him. He notices that he *could*—and sometimes "mistakenly" does—depart from the process, and he notices that he can depart, that he can conceive departure *because* there is an order. Like the philosopher who creates a system, he finds that the very act of arranging, of ordering, frees him from his product. In fact, the causal series which he lives in his work is revealed within a framework of means-ends without which causal series would be mere unarticulated possibilities. But Sartre is quick to say two things. First, what is discovered is a *partial* series, not the total determinism of neo-Stalinist Marxism. Where determinism is understood as a cosmic law independent of human wish or whim, determinism cannot and does not reveal freedom. Only in so far as the human project selects from among the innumerable interactions of phenomena can we speak of patterns, of causality, for instance, in any intelligible way. Second, the end is not wholly distinguished from the means, for ". . . the end is no more than the synthetic unity of all the means manipulated for producing it."[17] The end is revealed only in and through the means which together form an organic unity of mutually supportive elements.

The real, that which is impermeable to subjectivity, that which is expressed as partial order and as a resistance to be overcome through work, is revealed with a relation of means-end within a project. As Marx has it, one knows the world only through changing it, only through action upon it. Even the thought of the bourgeoisie, although advertised as contemplation, is itself the result of an action upon the world and is itself an action. But an *action* requires going beyond the current circumstance. It places itself in *opposition* to that circumstance. Thus, it is conceivable only as the result of the interrelation of an objective order and a subjectivity neither of which are reducible to one another. Here we can cite Sartre's by now famous example of climbing a hill. One must say that when we say that a hill is difficult to climb, or easy to climb, our locution is intelligible only if we situate it within the context of a plan to climb. Apart from such a project, the attribution of these properties to the hill would be the crudest sort of personification, but, given the project of climbing, the hill *is* hard to climb. It is precisely this sort of situation which frustrates both idealism and materialism. Materialism cannot speak of the subjective component. Idealism speaks of the objective component only in terms which allow some to utter the hilarious claim that the first World War was a struggle between Descartes and Kant. What is required instead of these discredited positions is an ontology which insists upon a relation of world and subjectivity so strong that neither is imaginable without the other. Sartre's text is direct, for what he insists is that we will not *appreciate* freedom if we do not give full play to resistance, that the ". . . maximum of reality, the maximum of resistance, will be obtained if we suppose that man is, by definition, within-a-situation-in-the-world—and that he comes to learn the stubbornness of reality in defining himself in relation to it."[18] That line constitutes an invitation to combine the "subjectivity" of "Existentialism is a Humanism" with the requirements of a revolutionary philosophy. One also recalls that a situation is brought into being only by the totalizing action of the human reality, an action which presents itself as being a total comprehension of the universe because the worker's plan is a total point of view. It is because the revolutionary goes beyond a given circumstance toward a future and regards it from the point of view of the future that it is *realized as a situation.*

Thus, to know that one is being-in-*this*-situation is already to be beyond it. Sartre asserts that it is precisely this possibility of transcendence which is called freedom, and it is precisely this which no materialism, even Marxist materialism, can explain. Conceived as object-men, humans might be understood to *respond* to prior states of the world and to modify present and future states, but no mere object could rise to reflection and, thus, no mere object could be in a situation. Although this contention applies primarily to an object conceived as an element in a material order, it is clear that the same would be true of a fully determinate order whatever its medium. The heady air of freedom so cherished by some of Sartre's readers again arises. But Sartre is stern:

Thus freedom is to be discovered only in the act, and is one with the act; it forms the basis of the relations and interrelations that constitute the acts' internal structures. It never derives pleasure from itself, but reveals itself in and through its results. It is not an inner virtue which permits us to detach ourselves from very pressing situations, because, for man, there is no inside and no outside. But it is, on the contrary, the power to commit one's self in present action and to build a future; it generates a future which enables us to understand and to change the present.[19]

This is not the free being celebrated in some of the plays, much less the model for the beardniks who flocked to the caves on St. Germain de Près and paraded as "existentialists." In the face of great adversity, in the presence of the ever growing weight of facticity, above all, with a clear consciousness of the contingency which infects being, the revolutionary must forge his future and forge his present in the light of that future. Man is that being forced to choose himself. That is the message of

49

"Existentialism is a Humanism." But he is forced to choose, himself, in a situation not all elements of which are of his choosing any more than the elements of the human condition are of his choosing. If I am born a petty bourgeois, I find myself in the world in that mode. Whether I accept it or reject it, *I must take account of it.* One who was not, as Sartre is, the scion of the petty bourgeoisie would not have had to pause here to account for his right to claim a part in the revolution, to show that revolutionary philosophy is also action and not merely a gloss upon the realities of the oppressed person's project. It is the view of the Marxist "Other" that when a member of the upper classes joins the revolution, his motives must always be suspect. The trials of this unfortunate person are dramatized in the figure of the troubled young assassin in *Dirty Hands.* Neither he nor Sartre can choose to have the Other abandon his suspicion much less his barely concealed contempt; neither he nor Sartre can disengage himself from "the absolute and insurmountable pluralism of freedoms marshalled against one another." The virulence of that ingredient in Sartre's circumstances is reflected best in the startling statement that the petty bourgeois is the victim of his own oppression, and thus, as an oppressed person, may be a revolutionary. The claim is almost sheer sophistry but it does point up the nonchosen elements of any situation. It represents, no less than Sartre's attempt to suggest that not all realism need be *directly* associated with the material, that relations with the Other provide at least as much conflict, resistance, and threat as do relations with the implacable forces of the sheerly natural.

To pursue this tack is to say again that the essay considered here is a clear departure from materialism and from Marxism in so far as it is a materialism. What Sartre offers is a philosophy of revolution, not an ideological accompaniment to Communism. A "Marxist" refused by his fellows, a revolutionary haunted by his bourgeois origins, a phenomenologist trying to reenter the world, Sartre shows us here what may be done by a

50

man who refuses to suppose that the chips are down. He offers not a philosophy of Marxist man alone but a philosophy of man per se. Marxist man—or at least man as orthodox Marxism sees him—is the product of his history and his environment. Sartrean man is always beyond his situation, that is, transcendent. That does not mean, however, that the human reality is other than its worldliness, its facticity. "Only a man situated in the universe and completely crushed by the forces of nature and transcending them completely through his design to master them can do this."[20] Through the analysis of the notions of "situation" and "being-in-the-world," Sartre tries to do full justice to the paradox which is the human reality, a creature wholly bound and yet wholly free and thus never whole. Sartre's notion is difficult. The language in which it is phrased is paradoxical at best and contradictory at worst. Some have read Sartre as the advocate of complete freedom. They are not mistaken as our epigram suggests. Some read Sartre—particuarly the later Sartre—as the advocate of the human reality as consciousness incarnate, as *nothing* apart from situation. They, too, are correct. But only Sartre fully asserts the conjunction of both views, only Sartre has had the intellectual courage to say that his notions are difficult *because* the human reality is difficult. This examination of some of Sartre's "popular" writing has shown that his commitment to the view that the human reality is something for itself and something for others is unvarying. It has also shown that neither of those categories is more fundamental than the other, that the question of hierarchy or ontological priority simply does not arise. If that is true, neither should the question as to whether Sartre is a Marxist *or* an existentialist arise. It should remain dormant because a *full* view of his early period makes the question otiose. What is now required is that we confirm and flesh out that conclusion through an examination of some of the themes of the "technical" work which dominated that early phase, *Being and Nothingness*.

Two

FREEDOM'S
BONDS

What can be said most truthfully about the issues discussed thus far is that they form a position whose major emphasis is not available to our ordinary form of reasoning, the analytical mode. In a passage which we quoted, for instance, Sartre remarks that only a being which is completely immersed in nature, completely submerged in the vicissitudes of the real and yet capable of transcending them, can be a being which undertakes revolution. In another place we noted Sartre's famous epigram, "The human reality is what he is not and is not what he is." In terms of the most respected of the varieties of the analytical mode of reasoning, logic, the second assertion is a self-contradiction. The first appears incoherent. One is strongly tempted to dismiss both claims or to play the ancient and honored game called "straightening him out." Both of these seductive responses should be resisted, however, if for no other reason than that Sartre lays claim to the title of "dialectician," and, whatever else is involved in that much abused designation, it signals a type of thought which tries to remain faithful to a subject matter which has negation and contrariety as constituent elements. To abandon a position such as Sartre's would be to reject a philosophical stance simply because it fails to fit categories other than those which it explicitly endorses, that is, to argue that "he's wrong because I'm right." To "straighten it out" would be to suppose that its claim to represent a crazy, mixed-up world must be false. Since both of these moves are philosophically and rationally unacceptable, we must try to come to grips with Sartre's contentions in their own terms.

But how can we do that without simply repeating and detailing the ambiguity it presents? We might try to do so by taking one of the contrary features and emphasizing it, giving it the strongest possible statement. If this is done well, it should lead to its own negation, for the movement of dialectical thought is said to be engendered by the clash of contraries. To emphasize any one of those contraries must therefore intensify the clash and bring the other into prominence. But which contrary should be chosen? Since our concern here is to bring to bear some of the apparatus of *Being and Nothingness* upon the controversy over the relationship of Sartre's existentialism to his Marxism, of freedom to involvement, it might be thought that we should select transcendence. One can say without hesitation that *Being and Nothingness* represents one of the most radical statements of freedom and transcendence in philosophical literature. But, for purposes of our argument, it is better to examine *Being and Nothingness* with respect to the limitations within which freedom finds itself. It is our contention that these limitations have been too little noted by those who contrast Sartre's earlier work with his later efforts and that those readers overstate the contrast because they neglect the constraining features of the world in which the human reality finds itself. We shall, therefore, try to emphasize freedom's bonds and hope that the emphasis will not have merely a cor-

54

rective effort but will lead to a short statement of the dimensions of freedom itself, both as a conclusion to this effort and as the beginning of the consideration of these and other relevant themes in *CRD*.

We begin by restating the position we took in the first chapter. Sartre tells us, for instance, that what is required for a revolutionary philosophy is an analysis of the notions of "situation" and "being-in-the-world." The point can be put more strongly. The human reality, for Sartre, is always being-in-a-situation. But what does that peculiar phrase mean? At a minimum, it means that a human being awakens to himself as being "always already in the world," furnished with a physical body, a social origin and status, immersed in an historical epoch, engrossed in dealing with the necessities of having been born, having to labor, and to die. His situation results from the fact that he *lives*, in his own fashion, the objective limitations which Sartre calls the "human condition." For instance, Sartre holds against the idealist Marxists that, in addition to a class analysis of one's situation, we must add existential psychoanalyses of individuals as family members, analyses like his of Jean Genet. The historical epoch also requires attention, for, whatever its sources in economic conflict may be, whatever response I make to it, the conflict in Viet Nam is an ingredient of my time of which I *must* take account. So, too, the bomb, the computer, long, hot summers, and other aspects of this slice of space-time.

The features of the life-world cited above are by no means peculiar to the Sartrean stance; indeed, the content is commonplace. We cite them precisely to call attention to what may be neglected *because* it is commonplace. This prophet of radical freedom sees the man who *is* his freedom as a man who is also caught in a network of social relations. Insofar as what a man can *know* himself to be, he knows himself through the eyes of the Other. Why some of Sartre's critics have given insufficient emphasis to this is a difficult question. One can understand why

Communist polemicists might raise the cry of "subjectivist" or "voluntarist" against Sartre. When the restraints of the Popular Front programs were loosed, the return to hard line Stalinism, required defamation more than refutation. But one is sorely puzzled when a loyal but unintimidated Marxist of the stature of Adam Schaff can casually toss off a remark of the following kind:

> The autonomous conception, on the other hand, rejects the existence of any superhuman forces as responsible for the creation—physical and spiritual—of the human individual and his behavior; as a result, it believes in humanism. One of them—exemplified, for instance, in Sartre's aetheistic existentialism—by rejecting heteronomy and construing its humanistic autonomism, takes as its starting point the individual interpreted as a spiritual monad (a monad of will, conscience, emotion, etc.). In an extreme interpretation, it is a typical Leibniz monad which "has no windows"; the individual is lonely, isolated, "doomed to freedom" or "doomed to choice," and has no help or assistance. It is true that the metaphysical concept of heteronomy—which the modern, scientific mind cannot accept without renouncing all its habits of thinking—has been eliminated, but a mere trifle has been lost in the process—society and the bonds that arise within its framework. And it is no wonder that the purely subjectivist and asocial pattern of this type of existentialism has encountered enormous diffculties, for it expects from the modern mind an equally great, although different, sacrifice as does its antagonist. Sartre, it is true, looks for a way out, and attempts to reconcile existentialism and historical materialism—but without success. The result is that the structure of his doctrine is far from coherent and its "original sin" remains.[1]

True, Schaff has the good conscience to speak of an "extreme" interpretation and to acknowledge that Sartre attempts to "reconcile" his sinful views with social realities. But why "reconcile"? Were Schaff one of those thinkers who reduces men to object-men, one could understand his implicit condemnation of Sartre's ontology. But the thrust of the article in which Schaff's remarks occur is to emphasize the need for a rejection and transcendence of Stalinist Marxism and this for many of the same reasons for which Sartre has rejected that standpoint.

The social bonds of which Schaff speaks are scarcely unknown to Sartre or unappreciated by him. It is Sartre who has
said again and again that the human reality finds itself alienated in the world where oppression is a fact so formidable that
Sartre confesses himself unable to write an ethics. It is not open
to man at this time to choose a situation in which oppression is
not an ingredient even though Sartre does claim that its present
forms may be surpassed and devotes himself to that surpassing.
Much less can the human condition be moulded so as to fit
one's desires entirely. After analysis, after synthesis, there remains that "opaque residue" which is the face of reality in the
world. One encounters both contingency and resistance in making man what he will be. In the light of a human project, things
reveal their "coefficient of adversity." True, it is only in that
light that the coefficient appears, but the word is "revealed,"
not "created." If it is proper to attribute the epistemological
characteristic of "construction," as the fundamental mode of
knowing, to idealism, and that of "discovery" to traditional
realism, then "revelation" is neither of these. The terms "constitution" or "positing" which were prominent in Sartre's orthodox phenomenological phase are much closer to "revelation."

Apart from human action, the mountain is neither hard nor
easy to climb, apart from the means-ends circuit, causal relations do not appear, but neither do these appear apart from *that
to which* human action is addressed. Reality is that which is impermeable to subjectivity. Men must wait for the sugar to melt.
Prior to acting, one does not know how the real will appear,
but we know it will appear, for there would no more be world
without the real than there would be world without consciousness. Neither would there be action, for effort requires resistance. Every limitation is, at the same time, an opportunity, or,
to put the point strongly but paradoxically, if a man could totally succeed, he could not begin. A reality which lay behind
the appearances would seem to be the sort of thing which

57

would permit one to speak of eventual success or, at least, of indefinite approximation. With this notion of reality, it makes sense to speak of appearances being a function of human finitude, of innocence, of original sin, of a lack which can be remedied or progressively lessened. Historically speaking, this conception of reality has functioned as indicating a set of boundaries within which man's efforts were circumscribed, providing the standard against which they could be measured, which provided a sanctuary to which men could aspire lest appearance be all. Without the limits provided by the real, no advance within or beyond appearance could be conceived or undertaken. Since this claim that an obstacle is also an opportunity is essential to Sartre's position, we quote him at length:

> . . . there remains an unnameable and unthinkable residuum which belongs to the in-itself considered and which is responsible for the fact that in a world illuminated by our freedom this particular crag will be more favorable for scaling and that one not. But this residue is far from being originally a limit for freedom; in fact it is thanks to this residue—that is, to the brute in-itself-as-such—that freedom arises as freedom.[2]

Further:

> It is by means of them (things-in-themselves) that freedom is separated from and reunited to the end which it pursues, and which makes known to it what it is. Consequently, the resistance which freedom reveals is the existent, which far from being a danger to freedom, results only in enabling it to arise as freedom. *There can be a free for-itself only as engaged in a resisting world.* Outside of this engagement the notions of freedom and of determinism, of necessity lose all meaning.[3]

Sartre's claim that resistance, limitation, obduracy are necessary to freedom is unequivocal. If one also notes that freedom, negation and action form an "indissoluable whole," then one must say that *because* man is limited, he is free. It would be less startling to say that the notions of freedom and limitation mutually imply each other. But it would disguise that which must not be disguised if we are to fully appreciate why Manser and

58

Warnock and others say that Sartre frequently exaggerates. It is no accident that Sartre's language is paradoxical. One must say that, for Sartre, the presence of the real in the world constitutes *both* a restriction and an opportunity, and we must remember that to talk of the various "senses" in which that claim may be cast always exposes us to the danger of untangling that which is intended to be tangled. To clarify Sartre's paradoxical language is much like "making sense of" a Zen koan—both efforts miss the point. To suppose that the claim that "the human reality is what it is not and is not what it is" is merely a colorful way to say several other perfectly "reasonable" things, is quite simply to misunderstand Sartre or to place his thought in a context which distorts it.

This contention that Sartre's addiction to paradox must be respected requires further emphasis, not only for its own sake, but because it is of a piece with several other Sartrean themes which support the position we are taking in this book. For instance, Sartre has never abandoned the view formed in his phenomenological period that knowledge is ultimately intuitive, thus, ultimately expressed in *description*. In *The Transcendence of the Ego*, for example, he tells us that the ego is given as a passive spontaneity which produces its states. He grants, indeed, he asserts, that the notion of such an entity is internally incoherent, but then he adds, "But we have aimed only at describing."[1] If what is intuited is tangled, it must be described *as such* and dealt with in ways that maintain the features which are intuited. Since, phenomenologically speaking, it is *what* the phenomenon is which guides inquiry and explanation, rather than the reverse, we cannot permit our predilections to lead us to an explaining which becomes an explaining away. It is not hard to make a simple thing complicated, but it is impossible to make something complicated simple without distorting it. Commentators frequently remark upon the attractiveness of Sartre's descriptions of features of the human predicament which have not always been noticed.[5] It has even been said that his work is best regarded as "literary philosophy," that even his "technical" works should be thought to be intellectual dramas or novels. What we said before needs to be said again in this context. It is a mistake to regard Sartre's *descriptions* as *illustrations*, and it is also a mistake to consider his plays primarily as devices to exhibit principles or notions already articulated in his philosophical works. If one must do business on the relation of his literary to his philosophical efforts, it would be better to say that his plays and his technical philosophical productions are different articulations of notions not wholly available to either mode of access taken in itself. On this reading, one would be closest to Sartre if one said that the literary efforts were more fundamental than the technical philosophy, but any such grading would be overdrawn. It is no accident that the portion of *Being and Nothingness* most commented upon is the fourth and last, that section where Sartre's descriptions are most obviously an integral part of his *philosophic* effort and also most compelling. Even the poignancy of these descriptions is in point. If Sartre is true to his own doctrine, one would scarcely expect him to write a book which was wholly *dispassionate*. Even granted the requirement of a purifying reflection which might provide the controls needed to avoid self-deception, a dispassionate account of a world dependent upon passion for part of its very nature would be curiously inappropriate.

To say that Sartre's work must be viewed in the light of its own multiple facets is not to deny that each of those must be taken on its own merits. Where he presents arguments, they must be examined in accordance with the familiar canons of philosophical polemic. But the total effort must also be taken on its own merits, and where description is utilized, it must be treated as such and not as a persuasive device or as the reflection of an understandable French tendency toward exaggeration. If it is paradox with which we are faced, we must deal with it as paradox. If the presence of the real is both a restriction and an opportunity, we must say so—baldly. We may even have to say that the presence of the real is an opportunity *because* it is a restriction. To do otherwise would be to suppress not only the irreducible diversity of the world but its contrariety and, thus, to undervalue the place of negation within it. That would be tragic, for what is perhaps most true in the allegation that Sartre is a contemporary disciple of Hegel is that it is Sartre who has taken Hegel's attempt to do justice to negation most seriously. To miss this is to miss one of the most compelling reasons for regarding Sartre as a major philosopher rather than merely a Cartesian rationalist lost in the twentieth century. To fail to appreciate the import of Sartre's tangled account of a tangled world is to miss both the need for dialectic and the nature of dialectic. If—as Marcel has it—there are regions of being which are intrinsically indefinite, a methodological technique like formal logic, which has definiteness as an integral part of its structure, must fail to account for that region. If the world around us "makes sense," then to use a device which makes sense of it is a proper procedure. But if the world displays a dynamic contrariety, perhaps even a dynamism *because* of contrariety, a mode of expression must be adopted, a method of approach must be devised which will be appropriate to the subject. Since Hegel, many Europeans have thought that dialectic was the proper method, a method which would itself display the generation of opposites which marks the world. To deal with this sort of world is to pay the price of nondefiniteness in reasoning and of paradox in description. That Sartre has chosen to pay the price is not an inadvertance but the result of a thorough grounding in the history of philosophy.

Such strong injunctions should be followed by an attempt to put Sartre's claims again but this time in his own philosophical language. A revolutionary philosophy, Sartre said, had first and foremost to account for the possibility of transcendence. The human reality must encounter resistance, a subjectivity must encounter *an* other. A subjectivity must also encounter *the* Other, that is, a subjectivity finds itself in a world which includes a plurality of subjects, an "absolute and insurmountable pluralism of freedoms marshalled against one another." That there must be a plurality of subjectivities is due to the need to account for the fact of oppression. Objects do not oppress, only subjects do. Man is not only the seducer of man but also his oppressor. Objects may stand to each other in the relationship of cause to effect, but only men can stand in the relation of master to slave. But why "marshalled against one another"? Even if oppression is so ubiquitous that it seems unnecessary to use a finely honed technique like phenomenological description to deal with it, its omnipresence cannot be mistaken as evidence of necessary occurrence. Much less can any of its various forms be said by a philosopher of transcendence to be necessary. To answer this we must turn to further Sartrean theses. This man who has been called "rationalist" and "Cartesian" might well have learned from his presumed ancestor that to begin to philosophize in a Cartesian fashion or in the Husserlian variety of that fashion commits one to making assertions about the existence of the Other by beginning with aspects of the self, however that self is conceived. Sartre's remark in "Existentialism is a Humanism" to the effect that in discovering one's self in the *cogito*, one also discovers the Other was said to be insufficiently explicated, but it does signalize Sartre's awareness of the place where he must begin. Descartes recognized the same necessity, but, because he had no doctrine which made a relationship of a mind to something other than itself possible *in principle*, he was forced to detour through God to acquire a ground for the possibility of the occurrence of something other than his mind and, therefore, for the possibility of

62

further relations—like knowledge—between these two poles. Whatever difficulties Sartre may have with this issue, he does not have this one, for the doctrine of the intentionality of consciousness makes a relation to the other not only possible but necessary. Sartre fully accepts Husserl's belief that consciousness is always *of* something which is not itself that consciousness or an act of that consciousness. This belief is reflected in Sartre's doctrine that the For-itself is the negation of the In-itself, a doctrine which we must attend to later. It is mentioned here only to say that Sartre has retained the notion of intentionality despite his abandonment of many of the other essentails of Husserl's brand of phenomenology. It is difficult to see how thinkers including Sartre and Heidegger could abandon notions as essential to phenomenology as the reductions and still claim to be engaging in an activity which could be called "phenomenological description." The possibility of that activity was dependent, in Husserl's thought, upon the reductions, but this is not the place to rehearse that familiar puzzle. One should attend, instead, to one of the reasons for the rejection of orthodox phenomenology, namely, that in fact it led Husserl to a position very much like critical idealism. There is no doubt that this result is inconsistent with Husserl's announced intention to introduce a realistic current into philosophy, an intention which drew so many enthusiastic young philosophers to his banner. But for a Marxist there was an equally undesirable consequence. Marxists categorize idealism as the ideology of the bourgeoisie designed wholly to support and advance their class interests. To one who does philosophy in the United States in the standard manner, it is a curious sight to see acute men suggesting that to "reduce" the real to the mental is a technique designed to convince people that God is in his heaven and all's right with the world. Nevertheless, for some of his students, only those portions of Husserl's work which were consonant with realism, socialist or otherwise, could be

63

retained. Sartre retained the notion of description and the doctrine of intentionality while, at the same time, employing them with respect to the world rather than with respect to the transcendental field. One result of that retention was to be able to reach toward the Other from the realm of the *cogito* without invoking either deity or ad hoc devices to ground that possibility.

But it is not enough for Sartre to be able to assert the existence of the Other in principle or even in general and this for at least two reasons. First, consciousness is intentional in the sense that it is always consciousness of *this* or *that*, never consciousness of something in general. For Sartre, there is no such thing as an acosmic consciousness. To suppose that there is would be all too close to introducing the idea of mental substance, perhaps even a return to Hegelian spirit. Second, the orientation of those who rebelled against Husserl's "other-worldly" tendencies was to the concrete, to the world as lived. Not only had one to begin from what was present to consciousness but from what was present to man. It is for this reason that the phrase "the presence of the real in the world" was used earlier in this chapter. Man is always in the world which is both his creation and his creator, and any access to transphenomenalities can be had only from the standpoint of the world. Sartre found certain human attitudes to be that aspect of *le monde vécu* which required the acknowledgement of the existence of the Other. In his now famous description of *shame*, he claimed to have portrayed a human response that could only be explained by the notion of being-looked-at. One felt himself to be an *object*. But one came to be an object only by being considered to be such by a subject. Since shame does not arise as a result of reflection, the existence of another subjectivity had to be acknowledged.

Shame is not the only facet of human existence which Sartre cites as evidence for the existence of the Other. It is enough, however, to allow us to pursue the question of the Other as part of our emphasis upon the bonds of freedom. Shame is not a state with which I afflict myself. It is another of the elements of a situation which are not there by my choice, although, like the others, what I do with it is of my choice. More generally, the object that I discover myself to be through shame is not of my own making. The Other makes me to be an object as the anti-Semite makes the Jew to be a Jew. I am suddenly aware of a dimension of myself which is not *directly* accessible to me. The Other sees me as an object, sees me in a way that I can never see myself. True, I can take the point of view of the Other with respect to myself as I do when I cooperate with a doctor in diagnosing an illness. I can even try to treat myself wholly from the point of view of the Other, but the inevitable failure of that effort reflects my inability to grasp myself directly in this fashion, reflects my being-as-object as an "unrealizable." What is more, I cannot rid myself by my efforts alone of the object status I have acquired. This is seen more easily if it is approached through a reflection upon the opinions of an other. Should I discover that some one thinks of me in a way that I find unacceptable, I can take various measures to rectify the situation. I can challenge his reasons, or I can try to show that my behavior "really" fits an explanatory pattern other than the one which makes it offensive to him. I can alter my behavior so as to make the presumed inference groundless, or I can attempt to coerce the Other to change his opinion. We all know how to talk and to behave in a manner which will largely disguise our real opinions or to behave so as to give vent to them in a fashion sufficiently ambiguous to prevent entrapment. A great deal of formal social behavior consists of just this type of stratagem. We also know that coercion is ultimately useless, for, although we may cause the suppression of some forms of expression, the available number of modes of expression is beyond count. Even if the set of expressions were somehow exhaustible, he who alters his behavior under the threat of injury can always regard another pattern as covertly expressing his opinion, or he can even go to the desperate extreme of holding that he retains his opinion even though he never expresses it. Thus, coercion is ultimately ineffectual against the opinions of the Other. But, if this is so, one *must* have the cooperation of the Other to obtain a change in opinion. I repeat—one *must* have the cooperation of the Other, *freely given*. The Other *cannot* be coerced. He, too, is a freedom, a subjectivity. I may try to seduce him. I may persecute him. I may even try to transcend him, but if I do try, and succeed, he will remain a *transcendence* transcended. The Other, that ontological scandal is a limit upon me. His view of me as an object is no more readily eradicable than is a particular opinion which he holds. His subjectivity stands as an unsurpassable limit to mine.

I cannot realize my object status because I realize myself as a subjectivity. That realization is no more an inference or the result of an inference than is my realization, through the fact that I cannot coerce the Other, that he, too, is a subjectivity. Subjectivities reciprocally limit each other—I am a limit to him as he is to me. But, even if this is granted, how do we get from the fact of reciprocal limitation to the situation of being "marshalled against one another"? Why should either of us feel that his circumstance is unacceptable? Why should the Other be viewed primarily as a threat and our relations be necessarily based upon conflict? In one sense, the reasons are obvious. Since I am my activities, since there is no human reality apart from the action incarnate, a limit restricts *me*. In a world characterized by resistances which can only be overcome with intense, continual effort, who needs another resistance as unequivocal as this? Furthermore, this resistance, this opaque subjectivity, is unpredictable even to the limited extent that is required to allow purposive behavior. Contingency is his fundamental aspect, contingency as fundamental as my own, for,

66

as subjectivity, he need not do whatever he does, at least as far as the particular content of his actions is concerned. Thus, I cannot deal with him as I deal with the *things* which resist me. At the same time, I cannot deal with him as a subject only. *Because* we are subjectivities, we necessarily see each other as objects. True, I realize him as a subject but not as I realize myself as a subject, for I realize his subjectivity only in joint interaction. I must always see him as an object. I cannot deal with him as an end *only*, although it is open to me to emphasize his subjectivity. We each bequeath to the other the status of having a self which is unrealizable, unilaterally ineradicable because it is not our creation. I am what I am not and, whatever I do about that alien self, I must do *something* whether or not I so choose. To use again a phrase which was used earlier, I must "take account" of this alien being.

I say "alien" deliberately because that term conveys both the sense of the mysterious and the associated sense of the fearful which my object-being has for me. "I—I could have done that!" is a cry not unfamiliar to any human being and a cry not infrequently uttered in amazement and horror. Contingency again appears and, for Sartre, that appearance is very difficult to endure. If I attribute to the Other, responses to me which are similar to whose which I have to him, if I expect from him behavior similar to that which I choose to take toward him, my unease grows geometrically. It is, after all, a human world in which I find myself alienated and oppressed. It is a human world which creates me even as I create it. Sartre finds oppression evil. But apart from man oppression cannot occur; thus the Other is seen as a threat because he is seen as the source of evil. But the term "source" is misleading, for even if one grants that Sartre has shown that man is the necessary condition for oppression, surely he has not shown that man is its sufficient condition. It is man who is said to be capable of overcoming oppression just as much as he is capable of instituting it. Man,

67

according to Sartre, is that being which is capable of transcendence, capable of revolution. Sartre has a ready response to this objection. First, to talk of capabilities which *may* be actualized is again to bring into view the contingency of the human reality, the freedom which it is, and thus to raise again the fear of the unpredictable, of the *radically* unpredictable. It is true that, as an ingredient of a partial causal series, contingency is a value for Sartre, for were the series dense both knowledge and action would be impossible. One should also note that *in conjunction with* some order, the expressions of contingency are often delightful, even fascinating. But it is only in such a mixed context, only in a world which is partially ordered, that contingency yields delight. When encountered in isolation—or at least in as close approximation to isolation as can be achieved—contingency is unbearable. It is a matter of intensity, of qualitative, not of quantitative, import. So, too, that locus of contingency par excellence—the Other.

That man cannot bear the full face of contingency for long is revealed in the famous sentence from *Being and Nothingness*, "L'homme, c'est une passion inutile." This statement has been discussed in contexts which vary from the profound pessimism it is said to exhibit to an attempt to identify the idea with the Christian doctrine of original sin. We have another treatment in mind. Man, Sartre tells us, is the desire to be wholly something. That desire is ineradicable, for it constitutes the human reality. One may eliminate any of the particular forms which that desire takes, even the "original choice of Being" which determines the style of an individual's life, but as long as man persists such elimination will only give rise to another expression. This is true whether we can clearly attribute the doctrine that some modes of expression are "better" than others to Sartre or not. This is true whether or not we can assign to him the belief that a subsequent stage in the procession of expressions incorporates the earlier stages or whether we have mere proces-

68

sion, mere *substitution*, as Maritain has it. The revolution, Sartre said, was permanent. Although we can eliminate the forms of oppression which we now have with us, although we can advance to a state in which man is not whatever his circumstances now lead him to be, no such state will be the mark of the cessation of the process of transcendence. What we do know is that man will seek to be God, will still seek to make a unity of what is intrinsically diverse—and will fail.

Notice that this characteristic of the human reality is fixed. In this respect it is perilously close to the assertion that there exists a human nature, an idea which Sartre has explicitly denied. But we must look more closely at what is meant by the phrase "human nature." Clearly, Sartre refused the belief that there existed a human nature which was (1) something apart from its various exemplifications although somehow able to be realized in them, and (2) remained what it was whatever the adventures of concrete human beings might be, and (3) existed prior to the occurrence of its exemplifications. At least part of the Sartrean objection to essences is that they may be understood to make individuals into mere instances, to make the idiosyncratic aspects of the concrete human being as irrelevant as the particular characteristics of a value which is substituted for a variable. The impoverishment of the real individual is also deepened if one associates this conception of essence with a simplistic doctrine of abstraction as the mode of its apprehension where what one does is seek out commonalities. It is not open to Sartre to deny human commonalities, nor does he do so. For instance, there is a human condition, and subjectivities must conflict. What one is tempted to say is that there are universal human problems but no universal human solutions. One of these problems is the inescapability of the quest for the Absolute which constitutes the human reality. Sartre has told us that man is condemned to be free, that even a freedom which works against itself is, nonetheless, a freedom. One

69

may also say that man is condemned to seek wholeness, to seek to be total.

Neither freedom nor the fruitless quest exists apart from man, much less prior to their "exemplifications." But there is a sense in which they are "fixed," a sense in which they remain what they are, whatever the adventures of concrete human beings may be. Any explanation of human behavior must take these features as permanent dimensions. This is not to say that one can go directly from what man is to a particular action of a particular human being. To do this would be to commit the same sort of mistake for which Sartre castigates the idealist Marxists in asserting that they immediately "reduce" a particular piece of behavior or a particular person to instances of some general principles like that of class conflict. Sartre refuses any notion of reduction but still insists that no particular case of human behavior can be ultimately accounted for without reference to the global view that man is the desire to be God. This hopeless quest is the massive correlate of the ineradicable fact of contingency which so impresses Sartre. To succeed in becoming wholly something would be to eliminate contingency, to unify consciousness and its object, to remove the refusal from the relation of *pour-soi* and *en-soi* which Blackham so elegantly described as "unmediated identity denied."[6] It would also be to cease to be human—which is one reason for characterizing this desire as the desire to be God. To remove the problem is to remove the human, although to remove some particular context of the problem might well be to become human.

One must ask how the relationship between this ineradicable aspect of the human reality and its various realizations is to be conceived. One answer is that they are one. That phrase, itself, however accurate, exhibits its own inadequacy. What seems clear is that the relationship cannot be between two definite, distinct entities. Sartre is much too aware of his philosophical antecedents to permit any conception of a general which might

70

lead to reification. His discussion of various collectives as "parasitic realities" makes this point specifically. But he is too well versed in the history of philosophy not to realize that most of the traditional puzzles concerning the relations of "universals" to "particulars" may be traced to one or both having been made too definite. What is recommended is that we conceive this common human characteristic, this inexpungible desire to be God, as the indefinite feature of an ambiguous or nondefinite field. The complex which is composed of this desire-as-it-appears-through-various-individuals might be likened in this respect to what Maritain calls an "intelligible mystery" or what Marcel calls the "ontological mystery." Alternatively, one might liken the relation in question to the sense of articulation in which one may distinguish but not separate what is articulated from its mode of expression. One wishes to say of this field what is well said of interpretation in the humanities. There is no single interpretation which excludes all other readings, but not every reading is acceptable. When faced with the claim that a work of art may be unequivocally evaluated, an aesthete will often retreat to the position that in artistic matters there is no final arbiter other than individual taste. But one often notices that a defender of idiosyncrasy will soon turn to expertise when confronted with an untutored opinion which is insisted upon on grounds of the sovereignty of individual response. The aesthete *lives* his world as though it were nondefinite. We concur.

This apprehension is reflected in all of Sartre's fundamental principles. It is reflected, for instance, in his claim that each human is an original choice of being, a choice which may, in principle, be discovered through existential psychoanalysis. He has gone so far as to say that the slightest gesture reveals that choice. His most impressive "proof" for his position is the existential biography, *St. Genet*. But, if one examines that work, one nowhere finds a characterization of Genet's original

71

choice which can be understood as that from which one might *deduce* particular activities. One nowhere finds a characterization which would permit us to regard a given gesture as an *instance* of that original choice. If Sartre tells us that Genet chose exile, if he tells us that Genet chose to be the thief that others made him to be, he does not then go on to describe evil or thievery in complete independence of the particular content which Genet supplied. To "account for" Genet requires the presentation of that original choice in its most general guise *and* extended discussion of particular adventures with scrupulous respect for the value of particularity and for the value of generality.

Some would wish to say that Sartre must engage in an account of the "dialectic" of the original choice and the particular gesture, and that is all right if one notices that general conversation when engaged in at length requires the addition of "concrete examples" precisely *because* it is engaged in at length. *The opposite must be generated.* Lengthy discussion of particularities must have a similar result. The original choice will be a response to contingency, an attempt to overcome the gap between consciousness and its correlate, an attempt to become wholly something. One may attempt to try to become a thing, to emphasize the *en-soi* as one does in masochism or seduction or anti-Semitism. One may instead try to become wholly a consciousness, an intellect, or wholly a freedom, a freedom which would not find itself in a situation. But to describe some of the behavior of an individual as an *instance* of one of those *kinds* would be as useless in itself as it is to characterize an individual as a paranoid or a schizophrenic. Not only are masochism and anti-Semitism significantly different attempts to achieve thinghood, but individual masochists differ as significantly from each other as do the categories.

While the form which the original choice of being takes in both its general features and its particularity is variable, the response to one's insertion in the world is not entirely a happenstance. To attempt to become wholly something while yet being endowed with a preontological comprehension of the impossibility of that effort is the most basic form of self-deception. But man is necessarily a self-deceiver, for it is his very ontological structure which is the ground of the possibility of self-deception. The actuality stems from the ontological structure of totality which Sartre sums up in the epigram, "Being is necessarily contingent and contingently necessary." The contingency with which the world is afflicted is simply the reflection of the original contingency of being. To ask why being must be contingent is like asking why the *pour-soi* is the lack of and the desire for the *en-soi*, that is, it is to ask a metaphysical question, and those are largely forsworn in *Being and Nothingness*. Being need not be, but since it is, much else is necessary, albeit contingently necessary. For Sartre, there is a high correlation between contingency and freedom, but it is equally true that there are necessities once a choice is made. The original choice of being is most unlikely to be altered. To alter it would be to effect the equivalent of the "radical conversion" of which so much has been made by Sartre's commentators. *But it is always possible in principle*, however unlikely. Until such an alteration occurs, however, much follows from that choice, so much that a thorough understanding of the actions of any given human being requires that the original choice be discerned. Much also follows which did not lie within the conscious envisagement of the individual in question. Being is contingently necessary, and when those necessities, those "objectivities," are encountered, much occurs which not only *was* not envisaged by a human being but which *could* not have been envisaged.

The case is not different with particular choices. In an alienated world, my choices have consequences which are what they are no matter what my intent and which range far beyond my capability to anticipate. In that world the very meanings of our words are sometimes stolen from us. That is no surprise to anyone who, like Sartre, writes as both vocation and avocation and who often writes for lay intellectuals, for an *audience*. When one's fame and fortune depend upon semipublic acceptance, one learns quickly that to write is to release one's apprehensions into a domain in which they do, and perhaps must, become alien, that is, they are cast into the realm of the Other. We cannot help but wonder how much Sartre was led to perceive the impermeability of the Other as a result of his literary efforts. Such resistance is encountered in many other domains and Sartre has exhibited it in various contexts, but perhaps no one is as likely as a writer to find himself constantly in an alien world. In any case, the realm of unpredictable consequences is our constant context and no amount of ostrich activity will let us avoid those consequences. To have chosen is to commit oneself to the consequences of that choice—*whatever they may be.* This is an additional feature of Sartre's claim that man finds himself anguished. Not only is there no ultimate justification for any choice, but the consequences of that choice lie in the realm of probability, and some of them lie beyond any calculus of probabilities or any codification of likelihood. One must act without hope where by hope is meant the affirmation of that which does not depend upon man.

But, even in the face of ultimate failure, we can do much. Sartre is a philosopher of revolution, a man who has claimed that there is no human reality apart from action. He is also the man who has claimed that only a being who transcends can *act* rather than merely function. The ontological structures which form the context in which man acts are "surpassed" in the sense that they, too, are nothing unless they are lived. One is inclined to say that they are nothing unless they are *realized*. But action, project, *praxis* all are notions which involve self-determination, self-origination. The limitations to which we have at-

74

tended in this chapter cannot be such as to make the human reality a function or an instance of the limitations, and "realization" is a term which often allows that kind of reading. Human limitations, ontological structures *as lived*, must also be understood as opportunities. Simplistically, transcendence requires something to be transcended. But Sartre's point is more profound. A situation *becomes* a situation precisely because it has been surpassed. Thus, I cannot be a *product* of my situation. This is not to deny that men are influenced by their social circumstances. Sartre fully suscribes to both parts of the doctrine that men make history precisely insofar as history makes men. His point is simply that the joint assertion of the claims that men ought to be different than they are and that they are wholly products of their social, economic, or historical antecedents is incoherent. That they are, in part, the products of inhuman forces is not a point which Sartre wishes to fudge. He has called our world an alienated world. He has insisted that the obstacles to a life that is fully free are such that full freedom is never finally achieved, that gains which one makes must be maintained with a constant vigilance and must themselves be surpassed when they become mere facticity.

What sort of being is required which would be capable of transcendence wrought in the teeth of such obstacles? Sartre's answer is that it must be a being which is not what it is and is what it is not. Were the human reality what it is, and only that, both action and knowledge would be impossible, including the knowledge that it is what it is. Only a being which is not what it is, a being which is the separation from its being, a being whose being is in question in its being, can act, and consequently, can know. Only a being which is in advance of itself, a being which is its possibilities, a being which is in the world as a *not*, can act and consequently know. This lack, this nothing, the project which makes itself in making its situation, and which is made, seeks beyond all particularity the impossibility

75

which is the unity of the *pour-soi* and the *en-soi*, that unity which the religions have called God. That impossible aspiration is not sought in a general way but sought in particular activities, and the particulars are malleable, alterable because they are what they are as lived. The quest for the general may be called the "truth" of the quest which man is, but the general is sought in the context of particular goals, objects, obstacles, opportunities, projects:

Thus we find ourselves before very complex symbolic structures which have at least three stories. In empirical desire I can discern a symbolization of a fundamental concrete desire which is the person himself and which represents the mode in which he has decided that being would be in question in his being. This fundamental desire in turn expresses concretely in the world within the particular situation enveloping the individual an abstract meaningful structure which is the desire of being in general; it must be considered as human reality in person, and it brings about this community with man thus making it possible to state that there is a truth concerning man, and not only concerning individuals who cannot be compared.[7]

The desire of being in general is irremediable, but the fundamental desire and empirical desires are not. Neither are the situations which result from transcendence of a local set of "givens." Human action can only occur with respect to *this* object, with respect to *this* task. While it is true that each of these projects or the project which is the original choice of being must be understood as occurring within the rubric of the impossible quest, the human reality deals with them in their particularity. Insofar as each of our tasks is directed to the achievement of the impossible combination, *en-soi-pour-soi*, it must fail, but insofar as each task is considered for its own sake as it contributes to the advancement of freedom, success, although transient, is possible and sometimes actual.

But one may ask—perhaps one must ask—how a man irrevocably condemned to fail can be spoken of as free. The claim seems paradoxical. *Precisely.* Man is also that being which is

76

condemned to be free which in this context means that he must act with respect to the compulsion which he is. Willy-nilly, I shall choose how to deal with the impulse to failure that I am. It may lead to despair. Many have called Sartre's views pessimistic or tragic. I may also choose what is called an "heroic" response or I may choose stoicism or libertarianism. Sartre recommends authenticity. But the point here is not which option I take but, rather, that for the human reality *there are options*. If one grants Sartre's assertion that man is a useless passion, that acknowledgement does not dictate how I shall respond to it. For Sartre, as for many who bear the title of existentialist, an encounter does not legislate the response. Response there must be. Even to persist as before is to respond. But which response is selected is a matter of a commitment which is ultimately unjustifiable. The grounds for that claim have been discussed before. Here one need only mention that the ultimate unjustifiability of choice is rooted in the same soil as the absurdity of the world as encountered, namely, in the contingency of being. In the domain of contingent being, conditions cannot be compulsions.

Sartre's response to this perilous world is to choose freedom while keeping the fact of inevitable defeat a constant presence. He might have chosen to deny freedom. He might, for instance, have chosen to live continually in self-deception. But it is not enough to say this. One must also ask of what such freedom shall consist. One must ask what it is to pursue freedom in the world in which Sartre finds himself. The pursuit of freedom must have a general aspect so that ". . . it is possible to affirm that there is a truth concerning man and not merely incomparable individuals." But it must also be particular. What we have again is the attempt to deal with a world which is ambiguous, a difficult combination of general structures filled by concrete circumstances which are not merely instances of those structures. The union, in short, must be *synthetic*, a union of incom-

77

mensurables if each one of the elements is considered as wholly definite, a dynamic unity of contraries if they are understood as internally related. One must try to speak of a commitment to freedom in a world of alienation. Sartre takes our contemporary world to be structured in a way of which "Marxism" is the most adequate revelation. We see that much is to be done by way of explicating the notion of "Marxism" because one familiar variety of that view, the neo-Stalinist variety, is not the adequate revelation of which Sartre speaks. His effort in *CRD* is to show what his commitment to freedom means under the conditions in which we find ourselves. His method was to focus upon the notion of dialectical reason as the bridge between man as a free being always in a situation to man as a social being. Our task is to show that if one reads Sartre as we have read him thus far, this focus upon dialectical reason has resulted in development rather than in conversion.

Three

THE DIALECTIC
OF FORMALISM
IN *CRD*

As is suggested by the title of his Marxist manifesto, *Critique de la Raison Dialectique*, the keystone of Sartre's Marxism is his conception of one of the varieties of reason, the dialectical. We think that a good deal of the misunderstanding of his position arises from the failure of his detractors to take this obvious fact seriously. For instance, the only way to certify a dialectical claim is to work one's way through the process by which it was revealed so that the course of certification has an incurably personal element in it although the conclusion is not binding upon only that individual. This is quite different from following a proof in the sense of a deductive proof, for conclusions achieved in this manner are said to be valid for *any* mind. What both logic and scientific inquiry demand is the minimization or the elimination of the personal element in the establishment of their claims. The interesting thing about an assertion made on grounds of analytical reason is not the origins of the "hunch" or the "intuition" had by the *man* who is a logician, mathematician, or scientist but the "objective" verification available for the conclusion. However great may be the human interest of the adventures of the men who discovered DNA, scientists, as scientists, find the discovery interesting because it permits successful prediction and control of intersubjectively verifiable phenomena, or, as some say, it admits of objective confirmation. Dialectic, in contrast, is always subjective but never wholly so. The "personal" element is an essential ingredient of a dialectical "proof," both as part of the activity of proving and as part of what must be "followed" if the notion of following a proof were appropriate to dialectical proceedings. To put the point in a capsule, analytical reason seeks conclusions which hold for any mind rather than for some minds or for some *given* mind. Dialectical reason is as uninterested in conclusions which are "true for me," and only true in that sense, as is analytical reason, but, unlike its counterpart, dialectical reason seeks claims which hold for some minds rather than for all. That dialectic includes this aspiration is not surprising if one makes explicit the implication contained in our previous description of the world in which Sartre finds himself. We called it "ambiguous" or "non-definite," meaning to denote by those terms a world which was a curious mixture of general structures or relations "filled" by individuals which were not merely values for variables in those structures, that is instances of those relations. A logic appropriate to that field would have to be just what dialectical contentions aspire to be, that is, individually certified as what is not *only* individual.

A similar contrast between the two varieties of reason may be obtained if we note that in logic one starts from beginnings which are only *beginnings*, from axioms, for instance, where in dialectic there are no such privileged origins. We do not say that sentences or formulae carry the label "axiom" as part of their very nature. We fully subscribe to the principle of postulational relativity. Our point is that within a given proof nothing is both an axiom and a theorem. In dialectic, this may well be the case. In modes of analytical reason like logic, the meaning of the expressions does not change in the course of the development of their consequences. Analytical reason is *linear*, one might even say one directional. In dialectic, in contrast, nothing is more familiar than finding oneself encountering the same claim again and again but finding that in going from context to context it has gone through a series of changes which result in a much different assertion than that with which we "began." Some have spoken of this feature of dialectic by saying that this mode of reasoning is circular or cyclical, so that Hegel could say that one could begin anywhere in the history of philosophy rather than being forced to trace its development by beginning at its Greek "origins."

Unless one understands these things, one will fail to gain a firm grasp of the type of Marxism to which Sartre is committed. One might also fail to see that Sartre's move from the writing of the period we have thus far discussed to the content of *CRD* is a development rather than a leap. This is particularly true of Anglo-Saxon philosophers like Warnock because the variety of reason most in vogue among them is the analytical. While we hesitate to say that any two philosophic enterprises are so diverse as to prevent essential understanding, the divergence between the European and Anglo-Saxon traditions is so great as to have led some wag to say that the English Channel is the widest body of water in the world. The typical European thinks that the British or American philosopher's fascination with mathematical logic, linguistic analysis, and the philosophy of science is quite understandable given his commitment to analytical reason. Anglo-Saxons often think that what the European calls dialectic is nothing more than an elaborate linguistic facade for mysticism born in the mists in the hills above Freibourg or frenzy born of hot nights on the banks of the Seine. Even our own annoyance with charges like Warnock's

81

stems partly from our disappointment at again finding an Anglo-Saxon acute enough to fully understand Sartre on some vital points but so immersed in her own tradition that she misunderstands some equally vital Sartrean doctrines. Since the major part of the audience for this book will be familiar with that same tradition, it would be well to begin our sustained discussion of the philosophic core of Sartre's Marxism by speaking of it in a context which will be familiar to analytically oriented readers. In that part of *CRD* called "Critique de l'Experience Critique," there occurs a section which is not only essential to the full comprehension of dialectical reason but which also offers access to Sartre's thought through particular issues familiar to Anglo-Saxon philosophers.[1] Sartre's concern there is the relationship between dialectical and analytical reason as seen through the consideration of "scientific" inquiry in general and the formal disciplines in particular. This apparently fortuitous occurrence of the combination of centrality and accessibility provides a clear opportunity to obtain a firm initial grasp of the notion which is the central theme in the rest of his book and, at the same time, to look at it in the light of a familiar, non-Sartrean frame of reference. We must be conscious that we run the risk of overstating what the author explicitly designates as merely one element in a complex yet to be developed, but all we need do to meet that requirement is to see that our conclusions are appropriately qualified by "situating" them in the context in which Sartre treats them.[2]

The context in which these themes occur is Sartre's attempt to explicate his claim that *la Raison dialectique* cannot be grasped from a point of view which is wholly external to the dialectic itself. In the earlier portions of this section, Sartre accused certain Marxists, Naville, for example, of just this error, calling their position "idealistic Marxism," "dogmatic Marxism," and "le matérialisme du dehors ou transcendental."[3] Sartre's general stance here is that the return to the pre-Hegelian idea of Nature, conceived as wholly other, forces these think-

82

ers to place the dialectic *either* in Nature *or* in consciousness, and that the consequences of that requirement are uniformly unfortunate. If one is dismayed by the conception of a dialectic in Nature *and* has only the two alternatives provided here, the result is inevitably some form of idealism. If one attempts to utilize the dialectic in the investigation of Nature, the result will be ". . . . elle n'est plus que l'idée vide de totalisation projetée par-delà des lois rigoureuses et quantitatives qui furent établies par la Raison positiviste."[4] Dialectical reason must and will be shown to have its proper sphere, it must and will be shown to be the only procedure fully appropriate to the sciences of man, but in no case can it provide anything more than heuristic principles for the investigation of Nature conceived as wholly other. That realm of inquiry is the proper domain of analytical reason.

Thus far there would seem to be merely a relation of otherness between the two types of reason. Each, Sartre indicates, has its own proper sphere. The characteristics attributed to analytical reason reinforce this implication of essential separation. Analytical reason is appropriate to a field in which relations are considered as being external relations. The effort is to break complexes down into their smallest or simplest elements and to understand the complex as resulting from repetition of the simple. Whether it be analyzing a compound into its constituent elements, finding a set of axioms from which one can deduce the rest of the sentences as theorems, or accounting for some apparent novelty, it is:

. . . the positivistic and analytic enterprise to clarify new facts by reducing them to old facts. In a sense, the positivistic tradition is so ingrained in us even today that the demand for intelligibility appears almost paradoxical. The new, precisely insofar as it is new, seems to escape the intellect; one accepts the new quality as a brute appearance, or, better, one supposes that its irreducibility is provisional and that analysis will discover the old facts later.[5]

It is important to notice the suggestion that the tradition which utilizes analytical reason is a *manner* of dealing with what is present to us. That manner includes the expectation, indeed, the insistence, that the new can be accounted for in terms of the old, that the complex can be reduced to the simple. It is as though "l'effort positiviste et analytique" were an attitude which one could choose to adopt or to refuse. In one sense of "necessary," that means that the positivist stance is non-necessary. Since necessity in this and in other senses is one of the characteristics which Sartre says the dialectic must have, we have a further contrast between the two types of reason.

To say that the analytic attitude is non-necessary is not to say that it is not compelling. One must notice again that this is the same attitude which is the root of the deformation of Marxism through the inclusion of a naive realism. One would expect Sartre to assert that this manner had some of the same seductive traits which he attributes to the materiality of the agent of *praxis*, of being both constant danger and constant opportunity for *dépassement*. One might even expect Sartre to hold that dialectical reason includes a tendency to convert itself into analytical reason, a tendency that it does not, should not, and perhaps cannot, resist. What Sartre does say on this matter is in part as follows:

We know also—and I shall give a better demonstration—that analytical Reason is a synthetic transformation with which thought intentionally afflicts itself; this thought must make itself a thing and be governed itself from the exterior in order to become the *natural milieu* where the object considered by itself is defined in itself as conditioned by the exterior. We shall see in some detail that in this respect it obeys the rule of the practical organism at all of its levels when it *makes itself* directed inertia. . . . Thus, analytical reason as a pure and universal scheme of natural laws is merely the result of a synthetic transformation or, if you prefer, only a certain practical moment of dialectical reason, the last, like animal-tools, utilizes its organic powers to make itself in certain areas a *quasi-inorganic residue penetrating the inert by means of its own inertia.* . . .[6]

84

It is useful if not necessary to transform oneself on occasion into the *quasi-inorganique* as, for example, when I try to make myself not unlike the *thing* upon which I type as I do the final typing of this page. To think, to rearrange, to retotalize is clearly as inappropriate to typing as it is appropriate to revision. Similarly, to think about a proposition in order to determine whether or not it is a tautology is clearly less appropriate than to submit it to a truth table or some other *effective* decision procedure. The danger is that one may begin to think and, perhaps, to live the world through typewriters and truth tables. That result cannot be entirely avoided but neither need it always be the focus of one's world. One can begin to understand the world through the universal scheme which is that of analytical reason. If one uses that variety of reason to great advantage, one inevitably comes to do so in part, but in what part is another matter. I do not for a moment suggest that Sartre is opting for a dimension of the human reality which always remains pure, untouched by temptation and in complete possession of itself. There is no path to salvation except through sin, and one is never saved once and for all. What I do wish to emphasize, above all, is that it is dialectical reason which *makes itself to be* analytical reason. While the process is complex and fraught with the constant danger of being arrested, whatever necessity is to be found will follow *praxis*, not precede it. Whatever may be one's decision on the much debated shift from the Sartre of *Being and Nothingness* and the Sartre of *CRD*, it is clear that he has not changed his view that the human reality is a vital, active force in the creation of its own destiny.[7]

But even if we accept Sartre's claim that analytical reason is to be included in the totalizing action of dialectical reason, we may still ask for further specifications of the relationships involved. In one sense, the question cannot be answered by anything less than a rendering of *CRD* itself. Like his master, Hegel, Sartre can say that the proof of his "system" is the system itself and thus that a fair assessment requires nothing less than a mastery of this totality. But—fortunately—Sartre pauses to comment in such a way as to enable us to make a provisional judgment concerning his response to a request for further specification. He gives an account a bit more specific than the one cited immediately above which asserts that to comprehend a demonstration using analytical reasoning, we must grasp both the analytic necessity of the calculus and its intent. Were the reasoning able to reduce the new to the old, it would still be reasoning and not mere calculation:

In fact, even if some rigorous demonstration succeeds in reducing the new to the old, the appearance of a *proven* claim where there was as yet only a vague hypothesis and, indeed, an hypothesis without *truth*, must appear to be an irreducible novelty in the order of Knowledge and of its practical application. Were there no complete intelligibility for this irreducibility, there would be neither consciousness of the *end* nor grasp of the progressive steps of the demonstration (either for the scholar who invented the experience or for the student listening to the explanation). Thus natural science has the structure of a *machine*; a totalizing thought governs it, enriches it, invents its applications and, at the same time, the unity of its movement (which is accumulation) totalizes for man groups and systems of a mechanical kind. Interiority exteriorizes itself in order to interiorize the exteriority.[8]

Analytical reason then must be a moment in a "synthetic" process? Why synthetic? If we suppose that the term has its minimum meaning as the relating of two elements which differ in some essential trait, then the reference to "new" knowledge provides the answer. Presumably, whatever is designated as new would by synthetically related precisely because it is new. But is that what "synthetic" means here? Sartre offers two indications: (1) the "connaissance" was—before the proof was written—only an hypothesis, but now it is proved, and (2) prior to proof, it was "sans Vérité" and—although Sartre does not *say* this—it is true in some sense after proof. Let us entertain a possible objection to this reading. Consider the case in

86

which a student is asked to do an exercise in logic in which he
is to prove some statement in the propositional calculus. The
student does not know whether or not it is provable, and let
us suppose that he does not know whether it has been demonstrated, even though the instructor is aware that it has. The
knowledge is "new" to the student in the sense that he now has
a piece of information which *he* did not have previously. This
knowledge, however, is not new to others, to the instructor, for
example. But many would wish to say that the relationship of
the proposition to its sytem was not new at all, that the system
implied, does imply, and always will imply whatever it does
imply. They would wish to assert that the only "newness" involved here was *psychological*.

It is necessary to ask whether this psychological account is
in conflict with Sartre's views. One has to be a bit uneasy about
the lack of Sartrean language which would permit the inclusion of that portion of the objection which refers to propo-
sitions implying each other in independence of our grasp of
them. That unease increases when one notices the continuation
of his remark, "...an irreducible novelty in the order of Knowledge and of its practical applications." It is always possible to
understand the "order of Knowledge" as "psychological," but
if one has any acquaintance at all with European philosophy it
is a bare possibility at best. The language of this objection indicates all too strongly a version of the same pre-Hegelian realism which we noted earlier was firmly rejected by Sartre, a
realism in which there is such a gap between knower and
known that one is *able* to speak of the "merely" psychological.
The opposition between the objection and Sartre's position becomes even more apparent if we take a second case, the case
which is such that neither instructor nor student know before-
hand whether the proof can be generated. Here there is no
question which can be settled prior to the proof itself as to
whether the axioms imply the statement in question. One finds

out whether they do only through the success or failure of the proof. One might say, of course, that either the axioms do imply the proposition or they do not, but that simply formulates the classical realist position in a particular domain only to argue later to a distinction between the psychological and the non-psychological which itself expresses the position.

Clearly, Sartre refuses to permit a complete separation between questions in the order of knowledge and questions in the order of being. The phrase "in the order of Knowledge and its practical applications" provides the occasion for that refusal if one remembers that, for Sartre, thought is but a moment of action. A computer, a logistic system, an axe, these are all means through which men live their world and deal with its various facets. To separate the system of implications from the knower is to skirt altogether too close to reification. A logistic system may well be thought of as a totality, but it occurs only within a *totalisation en cours*. The logic of the latter cannot be mistaken for that of analytical reason. Dialectical reason is precisely that which is to account for novelty not as a temporary manifestation of human ignorance but as a continuing feature of the real, a feature which is to be united to whatever else so as to maintain it *as novelty*, as irreducible. It is true that there are decision procedures for certain calculi. It is true that one can program computors to do the work of mechanical processes like truth tables. It is even true that one can begin to think and perhaps to act as do those efficient machines. One can make oneself to be a quasi-object. But note—one can *make oneself to be* a quasi-object.

This presentation of Sartre's views can be further specified if we turn to his discussion of a particular case of the relationship of dialectical and analytical reason. We begin with Sartre's own statement of the case:

In the perspective of the future totality, each new state of the organized system is in fact a *pre-nouveauté* and it is as such that it is *already*

88

surpassed by the unity yet to come insofar as it is not so new that it surrenders its intelligibility. I shall illustrate with a simple example of evidence which is both intuitive (and dialectical) and compare it to a geometrical demonstration. It is *obvious*—from the very first and especially to a child—that a line which encounters a circle at any point whatsoever must also encounter it at another point. Even a child or an illiterate will grasp this truth through the circle itself; he will say of the line drawn on the board: since it enters, it must leave.[9]

That this "truth" is grasped intuitively seems beyond dispute whether that be for good or for ill. If one considers to be intuitive any case including the empirical case in which a direct, unmediated apprehension of the phenomenon is asserted, this is such a case. Even I who am neither a child nor an illiterate grasp this content. But why the parenthetical addition, "and dialectical"? If only this context is in question, the reference to totality and to novelty appears to be the only clue. We have noted that Sartre tells us that it is only dialectical reason which can accommodate the inclusion of novelty as novelty. Further, he frequently tells us that action—that domain of which dialectic is to be the "logic"—always involves the "governance" of the present by a future which is essentially related to a past and that *dépassement* is an essential trait of dialectical proceedings. But to say these things is to explicate what is not *said* by Sartre, so, having noted the point, we had best defer decision until further examination.

Sartre insists that the mathematician will not be content with an intuitive certification of this kind but will require a demonstration, that is, will require that the proposition be displayed as a consequence of some formal system, a system which will enshrine and utilize analytical reason. He refers briefly to the kind of content such a proof might include. But what interests him most—and what is of chief interest to us—is the claim previously suggested and now made explicit that a change in point of view must be achieved *in order to be able to use* analytical reason. Much in the way that one must make

89

himself to be a quasi-object in order to act upon objects in exteriority, one must establish a domain in which analytical reason *can* be used:

> But what matters to us is that it destroys the sensory and qualitative unity of the *circle-gestalt* in favor of the inert divisibility of the geometrical "place." To the extent that the gestalt still exists, it is as suppressed in implicit knowledge. There remains exteriority, that is, the residue of the generating movement.[10]

If we suppose that dialectical reason is the logic appropriate to the original apprehension of this situation, then we have an example of the relation between the two sorts of reason which clearly makes the dialectical variety the more fundamental. Sartre's conviction that there is an indissoluble relationship between a type of reason and its domain should also be emphasized. The field which is brought into being requires a certain sort of noetic treatment, and that treatment brings the appropriate field into being. To ask which is ultimately prior to the other is to ask a question from the standpoint of analytical reason, from a kind of thinking which looks for beginnings which are only beginnings.

What follows these assertions is a full page of commentary which is bound to raise the hackles of anyone who has been raised on the formalist interpretation of mathematics and logic or at least on the strict formalism of Haskell Curry. We offer a paraphrase of that commentary with only minimal editorializing. Sartre tells us that the neglected *circle-gestalt* is not merely an inert sensible form but is a continuing organizing movement. The line has the same fundamental nature. The dialectical intelligibility of the theorem considered can be displayed by saying that the circle as the "abstract ideal of enclosure imprisons" where the line as unremitting passage breaks obstacles.[11] We grasp these movements in the very act of positing the design on the blackboard. The figure on the board is the result of a *praxis humaine*, it is a deposit, a *sillage, passé dépassé*.[12] The deposit on the board which is the circle is to be understood as the creation of an interior and as the exclusion of all else so that what is grasped is ". . . a generating act, the synthesis which assembles the palisades or which binds the abstract elements of space together."[13] The circle interiorizes the movement of the line in forcing it to submit to enclosure. The line resists such restriction by its very nature and thus, having entered, must leave. But in so doing, it ". . . réalise l'extériorité du contenu intérieur." Thus we realize the exteriorization of the interior and the interiorization of the exterior. But this synthesis of contradictories can only be understood in terms of a future totalization.[14] In contrast, what the formalist has done is to neglect —and perhaps then to forget—that to form a domain through stipulation is to remove certain intuitive contents from view but not to remove all.[15] By supposing that he has removed all, he can then make comments *about* logic or mathematics using the product of this forgetfulness as a model. One should not be surprised if one who constructs a logic to investigate a presumably nonconstructed realm (as, for instance, the natural language) begins either to see that domain as it appears with the compass of his construction or begins to take the construction itself as the origin of the activity, forgetting that a stipulation is the result of an *act* of stipulation. Understanding, however, need not yield forgiveness if what is neglected for *some* purposes, and rightly so, is neglected for all purposes, if what is not considered while constructing and refining a formal system is forgotten when one asks about the relation of that system to something other than itself. P. F. Strawson's correction of Bertrand Russell's presentation of the theory of definite descriptions is but one of a dense series of similar objections by analysts to the sometimes blind enthusiasms of ideal language philosophers. The general point is as obvious as it is important. What is not necessary for a logician or a mathematician to do his work may well be what is vital to a philosopher.

We can exhibit such a *philosophical* concern by reproducing Sartre's summary remarks in their entirety, and then conclude this chapter by commenting upon them:

Considering this simple case carefully, one sees that the sensory intuition is simply the generating act of the two spatial determinations inasmuch as the agent comprehends his partial operation by beginning from a double total *praxis* (of course, that is no longer true when the material becomes concrete—we shall have reason to speak of this at length; but in any case, the principle of dialectical evidence must be the grasp of a *praxis* under way in the light of its end). If this immediate grasp of the practical novelty appears useless and even puerile in the example sited, that is because the mathematician is not interested in the acts but only in their traces. He is not concerned to know whether geometrical figures are abstractions, limited forms of an actual labor: what interests him is to discover the relationships of radical exteriority beneath the mask of interiority which one imposes on the figures in generating them. But their intelligibility immediately disappears. One studies, in fact, the practical syntheses inasmuch as the synthetic action becomes pure passive designation, permitting the establishment of relations of exteriority among the elements which it has brought together. We shall see how the practico-inert discovers again this exteriorization into passivity of the practical interiorization and how in following this process, one can define *alienation* in its original form.[16]

This mode of comprehension appears not only useless but positively harmful from a strict formalist point of view. It is as though Sartre were demanding that we include talk about the practice of reestablishing farms obscured by the flooding of the Nile in order to understand geometrical proofs. Whether one calls Sartre's concerns ontological, psychological, or epistemological, they are clearly excluded from what has come to be regarded as properly *formal* concerns. Insofar as formalism is the vogue in discussions of the foundations of logic or of mathematics, Sartre's discussion runs directly against the current. Yet his language indicates that he understands the formalist attitude if not the techniques used. The mathematician, we are told, is not "interested" in acts but in their traces. He is

92

not concerned with the actual origin of his figures. Sartre nowhere denies that such a suspension of concern can be achieved and, in fact, insists it is sometimes achieved. The price for that success, however, is that intelligibility disappears, but the mathematician can always choose to pay that penalty. Although he begins with elements intuitively, even sensibly, apprehended, he need not and does not stay at that level. He descends to the level of the inert, the passive, the level of exteriority. I suggest that he begins in a realm which we have called "non-definite" or "ambiguous" to signify the mixture of definite and indefinite and then makes that realm to be more definite by selecting and maintaining that selection by a continuing effort. He constructs his field in a way similar to the fashion in which he constructs his self, and both field and self stay what they are only as long as his choice is maintained. Within the compass of that choice—assuming that the choice includes a commitment to consistency—there are "necessary" connections. To refer to an epigram of Sartre's which we noted earlier, being is necessarily contingent *and* contingently necessary.

But this is *Critique de la Raison Dialectique* and not *Being and Nothingness* which we are discussing, so one cannot leave the topic of the commitment to exteriority without severely modifying the degree of contingency thus far implied. There must be some sense in which that which "interests" the mathematician is not merely a matter of happenstance any more than the construction of a field within which the elements become possible sources of satisfaction for human needs is an accident. Exteriorization cannot be wholly accidental, nor can the concern with the exterior which is part of the process itself be mere happening. "L'intériorité s'extérioriser pour que intérioriser l' extériorité." One must account for the fact that the mathematician enters the domain of the passive and for the fact that he is sometimes arrested there. If alienation is to be understood in the light of processes such as these, Sartre's necessarily alienated man must necessarily involve himself in this morass and must do so "pour que intérioriser l'extériorité." Sartre must show that to be a formalist is one way to live one's world and that it or one of its structural analogues is part of man's destiny. He must show that it is possible to accept an account of mathematical proceedings which bases that activity upon contingency, upon what happens to interest the mathematician, without forbidding the inclusion of that account in a more fundamental explanation. Sartre allows the formalist to say that "philosophical" issues do not and need not interest him as a mathematician. But if one can consider this very contingency as a "nouveauté," then in principle one could include that enterprise as one of the irreducible moments of a *totalisation en cours*. Sartre's further discussion of the relations between analytical and dialectical reason sketches connections between them which would make possible a clearer view of the relation between contingency and necessity both in this context and in general. Our task is to trace the development of these keys to the nature of Sartre's Marxism.

Four

Sartre's attempt to incorporate novelty into order, to incorporate contingency into necessity, might well be examined by simply extending our previous discussion of the relationship between dialectical and analytical reason. But, despite our remarks to the contrary, that method might still have the disvalue of implying that the two varieties of reason should be considered as parallel or even as equally fundamental. That would be a disaster. When one speaks of analytical reason, one speaks of a domain in which it is appropriate to distinguish firmly between method and content. It is not by accident that among those practitioners of analytical reason, the philosophers of science, most are called "methodologists." Much of the work done by these philosophers requires a sound preparation in mathematical logic and in the techniques of inductive logic. Much of the work done by methodologists is as unintelligible to him who is unacquainted with symbolic logic as is much work done in physics to the intelligent but mathematically unsophisticated layman. In short, methodology requires a long apprenticeship, an apprenticeship almost as exhausting as that which is required to turn a student of science from one who is merely a perceiver to one who carefully *observes*. There simply is no parallel to these requirements in the exercise of dialectical reason. We do not say that dialectic is the innate possession of an arbitrarily selected individual or that excellence in its employment does not require long practice. Our point is that dialectical practice is not divided into two independent moments, acquisition of method and application of method. In the case of dialectic, the notion of *application* makes no sense, for the method and the content are not sufficiently different to make that notion viable. Since we shall hold with Sartre that dialectic should be understood as a logic of *action*, we cannot and should not try to deal with its fundamentals merely by extending our previous comparison of the two varities of reason.

Yet, we must deal with these fundamentals now, and we must deal with them with as close attention as we can muster. If dialectic is to be the ground for the reconciliation of contingency and necessity, it is through dialectic that Sartre can hope to incorporate the radical notion of freedom presented in *Being and Nothingness* into the further restrictions of the social world as laid out in *CRD*. What some of those who have understood these two books as poles apart have misunderstood is that Sartre is not merely trying to reconcile Marxism with existentialism by focusing upon a central Marxist theme but that he is knowingly, deliberately trying to maintain his commitment to a radical notion of human freedom in the midst of his growing apprehension of the impact of the Other as a *social* being. Because this is the basic motivation for Sartre's critique, we shall return to it again and again in as many different contexts as our theme permits. The most important of these is the one to which we now turn, to Sartre's "beginning," that is to his discussion of individual *praxis*.[1]

96

We put quotation marks around the word "beginning" because there is no merely individual activity which might be taken as a beginning which was only a beginning. Sartre starts here for considerations very much like those which we cited at the end of the previous chapter, namely, because he can show in a "material" or even a "natural" domain that he is faithful to his claim that "l'intériorité s'extérioriser pour que intérioriser l'extériorité." Sartre fully agrees with us that alienation cannot be a mere accident but must be a permanent possibility of the human reality. Thus he "begins" with an organism located in an environment of external relations. The organism is self-perpetuating, semiautonomous, a totality. Because the organism is in a field characterized by *rareté*, its cyclical form of renewal is interrupted. It *lacks*. The lack is lived as need. Although it is in itself merely a lack of elements which have only external relations, it apprehends this lack as need. Lack, then, is the first negation. Need is the negation of the first negation. It is also a surpassing of that negation and a vector beyond the organism itself toward the environing matter. It seeks in that environment for the stuff to eliminate the lack. In so doing, it (1) manifests itself as an organism (acts as a whole to eliminate a lack in a part of it), and (2) constitutes the environing material as a field of possible satisfactions (totalizes it), constitutes it as Nature, a passive totality in which it can seek further for nourishment, and (3) makes itself to be a quasi-object in order to act in a field of *extériorité*. In consequence, it makes itself able to be acted upon in that field. A human organism becomes a thing. He makes himself a thing in order to act. He makes himself to be a being externally related to the other elements of the field. But the radical form of negation is sheer exteriority, that is, quantity. Notice that this negation, like the earlier negations, occurs only within a totalization, in this case the totalization which results from the *praxis* resulting from need which establishes Nature:

97

. . . the man of need is an organic totality who perpetually makes himself to be his own instrument in the domain of exteriority. The organic totality acts upon inert bodies by means of the inert body *that it is* and which it *makes itself to be.* It is that insofar as it is already subject to all the physical forces which proclaim it to itself as pure passivity; it *makes itself to be its being* to the extent that it is by mere inertia and from without that one body can act upon another body in the realm of exteriority.[2]

But this exteriorization is surpassed toward interiorization because this *praxis* is governed by the future of the organism present as the end sought, that is, what is sought is a renewal of the organism:

. . . the temporal relation of the future to the past by means of the present is nothing other than the functional relationship of the totality to itself; it is its own future beyond a present of disintegration reintegrated.[3]

The notions of need, function, and *praxis* can now be treated collectively:

Need as the negation of negation is the organism itself, living itself as its own possibility by means of present disorders and, in consequence, as the possibility of its own impossibility; and *praxis* is at first nothing other than the relation of the present organism as a menaced totality; it is the function exteriorized.[4]

We can see from the above that negation makes sense only within a totality, and since man is the totalizer—at least at this level—negation comes to the world by man. Only within a totalization does the notion of resistance or blockage or even destruction have any meaning. As Sartre said elsewhere, the coefficient of adversity is revealed only within the compass of a project. But a project involves the presence of a future, and if that which is to be attained is not given from the very outset, then the very idea of an impediment eludes us. Apart from some totalization, there is indeed change, but there is no negation except in the sense that we could designate one stage of a

98

process positive and the other negative for some methodological cal purpose. Negation must be understood as something generated by the organism itself in the sense that only *for that organism* is the lack of certain inorganic material a negation. Negation occurs at all levels and stages of any *totalization en cours.* Any whole in which there are particularities is in contradiction with itself, for each of the particulars is a particular of that whole, that is, the whole is present in each part but insofar as they are themselves totalities, they are in opposition to the whole since, in being something for themselves, they are against the whole. But that is precisely the whole against itself. Similar remarks may be made of the various enclaves formed within a whole by virtue of the very fact that some enclave is formed, that is, the whole is in opposition with itself as a part and as the opposition of a part to another part. The point may be put more generally:

It is the existence of this non-being as a *relation in process* between the constituted whole and the constituting totalization, that is, between the whole considered as future result, abstract but *already there* and the dialectic as a process which aims to constitute in its concrete reality the totality which defines it as its future and its close. It is the existence of this nothingness which is active (*totalization positing its moments*) and yet altogether passive (*the whole as presence of the future*) which constitutes the first intelligible negation of dialectic.[5]

The occurrence of this negation is necessary because of the *totalisation en cours.* To be that type of totalization, this totalization must display a future possibility as its immanent end or destiny, a state to be achieved, to be actualized, *déjà la.* Any identifiable state of the process is such a concrescence. But it is nonetheless a process, a succession, and each subsequent state is the negation of the earlier either by replacement or by inclusion. Negation, then, can *only* occur within totalization and *must* occur if there is to be totalization.

Praxis not only constitutes the surrounding material as a passive totality but at the same stroke produces fragmentations of that field. "But this opposition comes to Nature doubly by man, since his action at the same time constitutes the whole and disperses it." *Work* consists in retotalizing this separation, in interiorizing it for the sake of an end in the sense previously indicated. Were it not for this characteristic of direction, work would result in the return to the original undifferentiated situation. But further differentiation occurs:

> This is what necessarily happens since the goal is not to preserve for itself and in itself the unity of a field of action, but to find in it the material elements capable of preserving or restoring the organic totality which it contains. Thus, to the extent that the body is function and function is need and need is *praxis*, one can say that *human work*, that is, the original *praxis* by which he produced and produces his life, is *entirely* dialectical: its possibility and its permanent necessity rest upon the relation of interiority which unites the organism and the environment and upon the profound contradiction between the order of the inorganic and the order of the organic, both present in the same individual; . . .[6]

But if it is true that action is dialectical, how is it that so many understand it in linear or even in causal terms? After all, science and technology are with us. Their very success constitutes a pragmatic warrant for the use of analytical reason, and to ignore or to refuse the conclusion drawn seems as perilous as to refuse the assumption of a domain of exteriority from which they begin. Some of the proponents of analytic reason, for instance, tell us that living bodies are simply complex cases of the relationships of simple bodies, that the organic is simply a highly complex form of the inorganic. They are not totalities at all in the sense which Sartre gives to them where they are said to be contradictory combinations of externally related elements internally related. How would Sartre respond to this claim? He gives a direct, if peculiar, answer. Neither analytical nor dialectical reason is equipped to answer the question as to why or whether there are organic totalities. Any hypothesis

100

on the subject is a matter of personal belief. If there are organic totalities, that is a sheer contingency, and the belief that there are is mere belief:

> What matters, on the contrary, is that if there are organized wholes, dialectic is their type of intelligibility. And since the individual worker is precisely one of these totalizations, he is not able to be comprehended in his acts or in his relation to Nature (nor, as we shall see, in his relations with others) unless, in each case, he interprets partial totalities starting from the totalization of the group and their internal relations to the unification in process, the means starting from the end and the present starting from the relation which binds the future to the past.[7]

For example, the famous law of the interpenetration of contraries becomes comprehensible if it is understood in the context of a totality, for each of the contraries has the whole as its meaning and through that each of the others, thus the secret of each part is in the others. But if one treats contraries as elements independent of any totalization, thus related only externally, the principle becomes a mystery. This is precisely what led Engels to his erroneous views. Because he conceived the field in which opposites occur as a domain of exteriority, his claim that they interpenetrate reveals itself as occult. Sartre is clearly of the opinion that a domain of passivity, a field of exteriority, is always consequent upon that of interiority. "L'intériorité s'extérioriser pour que intérioriser l'extériorité."

But one may still ask how it is that mistakes of the kind Sartre castigates here can be made. His first response is pathetic—their *praxis* is one that is not aware of itself! We neglect that. Then he launches into an "it is as though" type of discussion which repeats a good deal of what was said before but places greater emphasis upon the consequent nature of knowledge as related to *praxis*. We present the beginning of this move:

> At first, in fact, dialectical Reason includes analytical Reason in itself as totality includes plurality. In the process of work, it is necessary that the practical field be already realized in order for the worker to be able

to proceed to the analysis of difficulties. This "analysis of the situation" is performed according to the methods of analytical Reason and according to its type of intelligibility; it is indispensable but presupposes totalization.[8]

This indication of the "fall" of dialectical to analytical reason is fascinating, but Sartre does not choose to pursue it here. Instead, a long discourse takes place in which Sartre contends, without saying just how, that many confuse knowledge and contemplation and somehow contemplation leads them to continually express their dialectical *praxis* in the guise of analytical reason. Were they "conscious," they would see that knowledge is always the unveiling of a "champ pratique" by means of its end, by the future which is not yet, by nonbeing. They can always thematize their experience, and evidently this move is generally seductive. *But just how it becomes seductive is not said.* Much less is it said that this fall from grace is necessary. The fall is always possible, it is frequently actual, and it is avoidable or at least it can be recurrently avoided with the expenditure of great effort. One is tempted to stop at this point and say that Sartre has already indicated how, given organized totalities in a field of the inorganic, these totalities must sometimes yield to the passive element of their contradictory constitutions. But the tone of this section has been to suggest that this fall is necessary, that the way to the interiorization of exteriority is through exteriority, thus the fall is a necessary evil. We shall adopt that view without asserting that Sartre has made it out.

What has been demonstrated to this point is that individual action must be understood as *praxis* and as dialectical. The next step is to consider relations among men. This is not to say that in some occult sense of "original" individual *praxis* is original and interhuman relations are a consequent structure. Individual *praxis* occurs in a social setting and the previous consideration of it was founded upon a suspension of concern,

102

a deliberate neglect of relations to others which should not be understood as a denial of their fundamentality. The epigram which Sartre keeps repeating is that history makes men precisely insofar as they make history. But the analysis has now reached the point where the suspension of concern with the social setting of individual *praxis* must be abandoned. Sartre warns us immediately that it would be a mistake to shift to a conception of human relations which began to treat humans as *instances* of some social framework or grouping. To do so would be to place them in the realm of exteriority, to treat them as wholly external to each other, bound only by their existence in the same framework, ". . . which signifies that one is free to apply the principle of inertia and the positive laws of exteriority to human relations." This is to play into the hands of the "liberals," to play into the hands of the idealists, and it is all too ironic that certain Marxists make precisely that mistake. It is necessary instead to develop a theory of interhuman relations which makes the "subjectivity" and the "objectivity" of the individual functions of each other so that one may remain faithful to the epigram about history:

Man exists for man only in given social circumstances and conditions, thus all human relations are historical. But historical relations are human only to the extent that they are given *at any time* as the immediate dialectical consequences of *praxis*, that is, of the plurality of *activities* at the interior of the same field of action. Language is a good example of this circumstance.[9]

The field will be such that a plurality of individual activities will constitute it and be constituted in it. Sartre speaks of *praxis* here as not merely an activity of some given individual but as a general name for a set of such activities. He had previously spoken of the *"nominalisme dialectique"* but had insisted that to say that *praxis* is the name of a not-only-individual activity was to risk reification. The key to the inquiry concerning the status of *praxis* in general will be whether or not the same char-

103

acteristics assigned to individual *praxis* are also assigned to *praxis* in general.

The relation of individuality and generality with respect to *praxis* appears even more clearly in the domain of language. Each word has its singularities in the mouth of the one who uses it, and acquires further singularities through the variety of auditors. In a sense, one wants to say that a single word has been uttered and has entered the ears of a variety of people, but that seems a little spooky. Perhaps we should suppose that the word as a physical entity is a wave, since that gives a more intuitively plausible image than the conception of a word as a particle. If the word is unique and the hearers are unique, it is an impossibility to try to account for communication. The word—and possibly the sound—has both a public and a private being. It has to be around in some sense in order to be individualized. We want to say that there is a language to which each of us gives his own peculiar twist, and the auditors give our twist another twist so that the product is the nonprivate event plus my twist plus their twist. Thus, I cannot isolate any of the elements, rather, they are aspects of some same—what? Further, the language absorbs my twist and their twists so that it keeps changing in detail, although no detail disturbs the total structure. It's like a mountain which endures even while it is eroding. We do sometimes communicate successfully since the denial that we do, itself, presupposes what is denied. Thus, language cannot be made up of wholly disparate elements, although it must allow for some disparity, or communication would also be impossible. It is only in a Pickwickean sense that we could speak of communicating with ourselves. We have to say that the relations among individuals are as fundamental as the individuals themselves, so that neither "originally" gave rise to the other although at some given time we may speak of one giving rise to the other against the constant backdrop of the common fundamentality:

104

Languages are the product of History; because they are, one discovers again in each one exteriority and the unity of separation. But language cannot be produced by man since to be man presupposes language; in order for an individual to be able to discover his isolation, his alienation, in order for him to be able to suffer through silence and, just as much, in order for him to be integrated into some collective enterprise, it is necessary that his relation to the other as it is expressed by and in the materiality of language, constitute him in his very reality.[10]

The language is a whole contained in and containing each of its parts. "Each vocable is all the language actualized. Specification is totalization." A phrase is a particular totalization in act, spoken within and against the background of the whole. Again, we have the appearance of the most fundamental question in Sartre's book, the question which in this context might be phrased as "How can we be made by language precisely to the extent that we make it?" We do not want to make a fetish of either language or history. We want to avoid reification. Neither do we want to make either of them wholly subjective ". . . or we shall fall back into analytical reason and molecular solipsism." Once again what is sought is a realm which is an alternative to those that result from the belief that subjective and objective may be understood as mutually exclusive and jointly exhaustive of what-is:

In fact, "human relations" are the interindividual structures of which language is the common bond and which exist in *act* at any moment of History, . . . We do not encounter totalizations here, not even totality; instead it is a matter of a moving and indefinite dispersion of reciprocities. Our experience is still not equipped to comprehend the structures of this group or that one, instead it searches for the elementary tie which conditions all structurations: it is a question of knowing at the most simple level—that of duality and the triad—whether the relation of men among themselves is specific and *in what* it can consist. Like the rest, this must be disclosed in simple, daily *praxis*.[11]

It is well worth the effort to explore the notion of "a moving and indefinite dispersion of reciprocities." Are there discern-

ible, partially specifiable relations between individuals understood to be concrete enough to be numbered in a domain which
is not itself wholly specified and not, one suspects, wholly specifiable? Can we move from the display of the dialectical structure of individual *praxis* to a similar treatment of intersubjec-
tive activity in its most ordinary setting? The daily world is
what we earlier termed a non-definite or ambiguous domain.
So is the language of that world. Part of the reason for the rejection by analysts of the positivist insistence upon the construction and use of an artificial language was precisely that
there were understandings which were inherently indefinite
but not for that reason noetically useless. Their exploration of
the realm of ordinary language is deliberately piecemeal or
should have been given Ludwig Wittgenstein's inspiration.
Austin called it "field work in philosophy." Sartre's exploration
is more systematic but not in the sense that the positivist move
or the traditional philosopher's addiction to procedures which
result in deductive structures is systematic. Both of these philosophical positions involve the use of analytical reason. Sartre's
claim is that particularity and generality can only be reconciled
through dialectical reason, the variety of reason that can accommodate man's singularity and his social being.

For the context of this effort, Sartre chose the now famous
example of standing at the window of a hotel in which he is
vacationing and seeing a construction worker and a gardener
separated from each other by a high wall. He is aware of them
at first as *not* himself and is aware of himself as *not* either of
them. But that awareness includes a comprehension of them
in terms of their goals, a comprehension even more fundamental than that of them as men, for they are apprehended
first as a gardener and a construction worker just as Sartre is
apprehended as an "estivant":

At first they can be revealed only on an undifferentiated background of
synthetic relations which maintains me with them in actual immanence;

106

I cannot oppose their ends to mine without recognizing them as ends. The foundation of comprehension is complicity in principle with every enterprise—even if one must later combat or even condemn that complicity. . . .[12]

It is in terms of their ends that this group is apprehended, not only those immediately apparent but those present to them because they are members of society, a society present to Sartre in the conditioning which his social situation imposes upon his perception. Once again we have the presentation of recurrent themes, comprehension in terms of ends, in terms of a future, and inclusion of all agents in a social whole. Familiar themes continue:

On the other hand, each negation is a relation of interiority. By that I mean that the reality of the *Other* affects me in the depths of my existence insofar as *it is not* my reality.[13]

An internal relation like this is, among other things, a relation in which a modification of one of the terms produces a modification of the other. In discovering the others in my field of perception, I am revealed as an "estivant" in being revealed as *not* a gardener. The field itself in which we are thus organized appears to admit of such reorganizations: "Chaque chose supporte de toute son inertie l'unité particuliére qu'une action aujourd'hui disparue lui à imposée . . ."[14] But I see these others not only as objects among other objects but as like me in being themselves centers of organization, agents of *praxis*. Sartre uses his familiar phrase "perspectives de fuite." One usually says that one apprehends oneself or the world from his own point of view in a way that he cannot apprehend others, a way so different that one can only *infer* the subjectivity of the other from behavioral cues. Sartre insists that I apprehend others as subjects, as agents. This, he asserts, is an apprehension of their existence as subjects, not an inference from perceptual data. Further, it is an apprehension that has a negative aspect because the other is presented as a subjectivity, but I do not see his

107

world as he sees it just because I, too, am an agent. So to speak, I am always *here* and never *there*. I apprehend him as the sort of thing which is here but, unlike myself, is here over there. To use Sartre's earlier language, my world hemorrhages, leaks away.

The field in which these negations are internal is made to be through the perception of the man at the window, but Sartre is anxious to deny that it is therefore subjective. In this he remains faithful to his earlier view that the world we live is a composite of living and that which is lived, that the mountain is hard to climb within the project of a human being, and only therein, but *it* is hard to climb. To use the jargon, the coefficient of adversity is revealed only within the compass of a project—but it is nevertheless *revealed*. The relationships in which these men appear are objective according to Sartre although that term must not be taken in its usual realist sense. The only real relation which can hold apart from human apprehension is contiguity, ". . . that is, co-existence in exteriority." But the relationship which we are considering between the workmen is ignorance, and ". . . certainly these reciprocal ignorances would not attain to objective existence without me: the very notion of ignorance supposes a third who questions and who already knows. . . ."[15] The relationship does not appear for the third but by him. In determining the workers as ignorant of each other, Sartre is determined by them:

Objectively designated by them as an Other (other class, other profession, etc.) in my very subjectivity, in interiorizing this designation, I make myself the objective domain where these two persons realize their mutual dependence *beyond* me. Let us be careful not to reduce this mediation to a subjective impression: it is not necessary to say that the two laborers are ignorant of themselves *for me*. They are ignorant of each other *by me* and to the exact extent that I become *by them* that which I am.[16]

Now we have the appearance of a new level of relationship.

108

My act of perception as *praxis* organizes a *champ pratique* in the process of which I exteriorize my interiority. I am now the object I have made myself to be in order to achieve purchase upon the domain of materiality. But because these others, these "perspectives of flight" are in the field, I make them to be quasi-objects insofar as I am made by them to be a quasi-object. There is revealed a multiplicity of totalizations each one of which is not the other and each one of which is made to be an object doubly, that is, both by his own *praxis* and by his inclusion in the *praxis* of another. There is revealed a common domain of *praxis* brought into being by the plurality of unifications which also determine each other:

> The plurality of these centers which are doubly denied at the level of practical unification becomes a plurality of dialectical movements but this plurality in exteriority is interiorized in the sense that it qualifies each dialectical process in interiority and for this unique reason, dialectical development can only be grasped from within and by dialectical qualifications (that is, by the ensemble organized synthetically).[17]

We have arrived at a singularly different stage from that with which we began. There we considered the relation of the abstract individual to the surrounding world. He was portrayed as exteriorizing himself in it in order to act upon it thereby paying the penalty of being able to be acted upon. Now we are describing the existence within the field brought into being by a certain *praxis*—perceptive in this case—of not wholly material entities, presumably humans. We say "presumably" because Sartre says that they are not presented as men but as agents pursuing ends, making their world and being made by it. Each of the individuals in this field is affected by virtue of being unified by the field even though they are apprehended as centers of flight on the basis of the thesis from *Being and Nothingness* that I am what the Other takes me to be and he is what I take him to be. But to acknowledge them as like me is to acknowledge that they make me to be an object by virtue of

109

the activity in which I make them objects. The additional objective aspects which I thus acquire means that my "subjectivity" is now an "objectivité vivante," thus the occurrence of others is a necessary condition of any further exteriorization on my part. My interiority now includes what the other makes me to be. The external plurality is a condition of interiorization and of subsequent exteriorization *pour que interioriser*. But externality was said to be a negative relation. The Hegelian thesis that negation is a relation is assimilated by Sartre. To say, "I am not Joe Zilch," is to assert that I am in relation to Joe Zilch. At its extreme limit, Sartre has said, negation is exteriority—quantity. But exteriority is not the only negation involved here. Each one is not the other in a manner "active et synthétique" *since* not to be someone is to make of them an object or a means to my ends. To do this is to limit them in the sense that they are themselves totalizers. It is also to limit them in the sense that they now have something to account for which they need not have envisaged but which they are forced to respond to, that is, whatever I make them to be. Finally, because I am an agent, I conceal from them that aspect of the world which is unveiled in my project. Not only am I partially opaque to them—since they must see me as I never live myself—but I bring into being an aspect of the world which is inaccessible to them in principle. Nevertheless, "Cette négation est d'intériorité mais non totalisante." *D'intériorité* because negation can only occur within a totality, in this case a *champ pratique*, and because part of what I am is *not* the other. The relation is also synthetic and dialectical—synthetic because very different elements are nonetheless essentially bound to each other, dialectical because the relations exhibit the traits previously grouped under that title. But they are not totalizing. Why? Because a *totalisation en cours* cannot itself be totalised? Sartre says that. It sounds a little like Kant's passive synthesis.

What we have unquestionably learned from these analyses is as follows. The fundamental human relation is that of reci-

110

procity although that relation is intimately bound up with a tertiary relation, for instance, bound to a tertiary for its revelation. Reciprocity implies the following:

1. that the Other should be a means to the exact extent that I am a means myself, that is to say that he should be a means to a transcendent end and not *my* means; 2. that I recognize the Other as *praxis*, that is, as totalization in process and at the same time that I integrate him as an object into my totalizing project; 3. that I recognize his movement toward his own ends in the very movement by which I project myself towards mine; 4. that I disclose myself as object and as the instrument of his ends by the very act which constitutes him as an objective instrument for my ends.[18]

This restatement of the notion of reciprocity stresses a further aspect which is fundamental enough to be stated explicitly. A binary relation obtains against the background of a social milieu which is internally related to matter. All relationships of men including this most fundamental relation are mediated through materiality, through *praxis*, through the *totalisation en cours*, through changing the world. This is an extension of Sartre's previous discussion of the externalization of a single organism in a surrounding material environment in order to interiorize. The point is underscored through Sartre's treatment of the Kantian recommendation that we treat others as ends in themselves. Sartre tells us that the individual cannot treat his present self as an end in itself but can only use it as a means to a future self which is itself the goal of the present activity sought through embodiment in matter and manipulation of matter. For this reason, no self, mine or the Other's, can be treated in accordance with the Kantian recommendation. Here, as in *The Transcendence of the Ego*, Sartre holds that one's self is "in the world," a self to be created, and in that very act of creation to be surpassed. The term "world" has quite a different meaning for Sartre here than it had in his orthodox phenomenological period, but the fundamental structures are familiar.

Reciprocity is a human relation but nontotalizing. It tends

111

toward unity but never realizes the degree of integration which characterizes totality, and this for several reasons. First, reciprocity is a relationship between *two* people, that is, entities externally related whose relationship cannot be made wholly internal. These relations ". . . sont des adhérences multiples entre les hommes et qui maintennent une societé à l'état collodial." The phenomenological existentialist shows through in these lines, and it is not mere happenstance that Sartre concludes this section with the claim that his account thus far is sufficient for the explication of noninstitutionalized human relations but not for human relations as firmly etched as groups, nations, or societies. As we all know, it is perfectly possible to neglect the influence of such structures upon each other for a long time and, in consequence, to live a world in which such structures are not apprehended. Perhaps it would be better to say that they are apprehended only as part of a rather hazy general background which comes into focus intermittently, for instance, when we have to get a new driver's license. To have noted that this is the sort of realm in which we initially find ourselves, and to have proceeded to explore that domain *in its own terms* instead of looking immediately for the order concealed "in" it or "behind" it, is one of the prime virtues of investigation guided by phenomenological training. We must watch carefully how Sartre proceeds when he advances to the treatment of the status of more determinate social and historical structures. Perhaps, as he suggests, that story cannot be told well until the second volume of *CRD* appears, but since he works here as though part of the factors displayed were the foundation of all else, we must hold him responsible in his own terms for a powerful justification for any serious modification of that claim. The precise statement of Sartre's position becomes vital, so we quote him at length:

Thus each one lives in the absolute interiority of a relation without unity; his concrete certitude is a mutual adaptation in separation, it is the existence of a relationship to a double nucleus which he can never

112

grasp in its totality; this disunion in solidarity (positive or negative) results from excess rather than from lack; it is produced, in fact, by the existence of two synthetic unifications which are rigorously equivalent. We encounter here an object which is real and material but ambiguous; the terms of the relation can neither take account of themselves as discrete quantities nor can they realize their unity effectively. The unity of these epicenters, in fact, can only be realized in a totalization performed from without by a third.[19]

Sartre quite correctly insists that this lack of integration is lived by the members of the dyad as a negation internal to reciprocity. We say "quite correctly" in the sense that to go beyond reciprocity he must begin with an immanent characteristic, he must find the motive for transcendence as an inherent structure of the beginning. Otherwise he will fall into the "solipsisme moléculaire" which he previously rejected or be forced like Descartes to appeal to an ad hoc principle which has as its foundation only the need to bring together what he has put asunder. We are told that this lack is lived as an "inquietude," as "une deficience obscure," that ". . . the reciprocal relation is haunted by its unity as by an insufficiency of being which transforms it in its original structure." When Kant wanted to get beyond immanence, he cited as his vehicle that aspect of some organized sensations of being beyond the control of the will, as being "given." Sartre cites negation, which suggests that he has learned something from Hegel, but it is a *lived* negation which suggests that he has also learned something from phenomenology. In his own language, these points are as follows:

. . . and this *uneasiness* of reciprocity is in its turn intelligible as the moment when the dialectic produces in each the experience of the dialectic of the Other as a check imposed in and by the synthetic effort itself on the project of totalization.[20]

The encounter in this moment is not unlike those which Sartre has portrayed so vividly elsewhere, so vividly that, in concert with many others, he has given the term "existential" a currency which is startling and sometimes dismaying. Here, as in

113

the more familiar contexts of encounter, the awareness itself does not determine a response. The members of the dyad may assume their situation or may fall back into the absurd, into an inessential moment of a false totality. But that awareness may enable the members to realize the internal relation which they are to the third.

The outline of the relations of the most fundamental elements of dialectic, as the order of individual *praxis* which this chapter presents may be concluded by an explicit discussion of the relation of the third to the dyad. Let us consider the setting first:

> Because, as we have seen, the third discloses to itself the reciprocity which is enclosed around it in denying it in order to seek it again through its own insufficiency; in this sense, the relation of the thirds among themselves—insofar as it is absorbed in mediating a reciprocal relation—is a separation which postulates reciprocity as the fundamental bond among men, *but* lived reciprocity always returns to the third and in its turn reveals the tertiary relation as its foundation and its achievement.[21]

Sartre asks us to consider a circumstance in which two workers are observed by an efficiency expert interested in improving their performance. In the light of his concern, he becomes aware of the rhythm of their activity as an end, a grasp which they do not have. He grasps it as the objective end of the other and as that which can be used as a means to his own end. In this apprehension he reveals that end as an entity imposed upon them by the materially based society in which they live. The rhythm was not their end in their reciprocal relation but becomes their end through the *praxis* of the third. A "metamorphosis" has happened. The objectivity of this end escapes direct apprehension by the workers but is related to them as an end to be achieved and is maintained as a structure of the world through their *praxis*:

> Objectively and *by* the third, the independence of the end transforms

114

reciprocity into a conjugation of movement, the mutual adaptation into internal auto-determination of *praxis*; it metamorphosizes a double action into a single event which subordinates the two workers as secondary structures whose particular relations depend upon global relations and who communicate between themselves through the mediation of the whole. This living totality which includes men, their objects and the material which they work is at the same time the event as temporalization of the objective imperative of the end (from future to present) as the concrete unity of the event. In this moving totality, subjectivities are enveloped as significations which are necessary and unfathomable; but they are defined as a relation common to the transcendent end and not as each grasping his own end in a reciprocity of separation; thus, in their objective significations, having become homogeneous, are rejoined and are grounded in the grasp of the transcendent imperative.[22]

The individual subjectivity becomes simply the specification, the concretization, of a general, amorphous subjectivity whose function is just to interiorize the objective end. Individual subjectivity *at this stage* becomes inessential. *This* individual becomes the anonymous "one." What we have is an embryonic stage of group relationships, the social beginning of the phenomenon which leads men to be able to treat themselves and to be treated largely as objects, so that, as Marcel has it, a man can all but become his functions. We have the beginning of the passage from individuality to anonymity:

By his mediation, the third reanimates the objective significations which are already inscribed in things and which constitute the group as a totality. These crystallized significations already represent the anonymous *praxis* of the Other and manifest a formed unveiling by means of matter. By recalling them, the third is made mediator between objective thought as Other and concrete individuals; by means of him a fixed universality *constitutes* them by its very operation.[23]

By means of a third, the reciprocal duality becomes a material unity through a relationship which is interior, since the third is modified by his participation, but not reciprocally. Sartre says, ". . . cette relation ne peut que lier sans unifier . . . la dyade devient équipe non en produisant sa totalité mais en la subissant d'abord comme détermination de l'être."[24]

It is necessary to conclude by emphasizing that the relation between dyad and third is not reciprocal, for there may in fact result an hierarchical arrangement in which each member in his turn becomes a third. Of course, each individual is a third with respect to *some* others but whether he is a third with respect to *these* others is another question, a question which only history will decide. That there is a plurality of acting organisms is beyond question for Sartre. The exteriority exhibited by the fact of plurality is grounded in the material base of the society in which we find inter-individual action:

> But although the natural dispersion can only be the abstract meaning of the real, that is, the social dispersion, it is this negative element of mechanical exteriority which, in the framework of a given society, always conditions the strange relation of reciprocity which at the same time denies plurality by the cohesivness of activities and denies unity by the plurality of recognitions and the relation of the third to the dyad is determined as exteriority in pure interiority.[25]

Dyad *and* third, interiority *and* exteriority, particularity *and* generality—Sartre insists upon a union of opposites at the close of his discussion of individual *praxis* just as he did at the outset. He insists because he is sternly faithful to his claim that the complicated cannot be made simple, that the world must be treated in its own terms rather than being "straightened out" by the imposition of some neat scheme. We have taken the liberty of treating Sartre in his own terms only to the extent of presenting the skeletal framework of his stance. What we needed was a close statement of the basis of his treatment of dialectical reason so that we might achieve a rapid extension of our concern with it as the philosophic core of his Marxism. What must now be done is to build upon this foundation by turning back to the notion of reciprocity as the keystone of that variety of reason which is both in and of the world.

116

Five

CHESS
À LA SARTRE

The relation called reciprocity to which Sartre's discussion of individual *praxis* leads is indeed strange. It is a relationship which undergoes regular metamorphoses but which retains the identity of the individual despite making his relationship to the Other a fundamental aspect of himself. This theme is scarcely new in Sartre's thought as is indicated by the fact that being-for-others was a fundamental category in *Being and Nothingness*. But the very order in which Sartre discussed the various modes of being can lead one to believe that the *pour-soi* is a more fundamental category. No such response is possible in reading the sections of *CRD* to which we have just attended and that may well be one of the reasons which contribute to the belief of some that Sartre has undergone a radical conversion. But what is of greater interest here is the idea of reciprocity in itself, for, unless Sartre can establish it, his attempt to integrate contingency into necessity will fail. We have said elsewhere that Sartre is perfectly aware that his insistence upon the autonomy of the individual human creates great difficulties when dealing with the human in terms of intersubjectivity. Sartre's difficulty was so great that it led Merleau-Ponty to say that there was a place in Sartre's position for subjectivity but that his emphasis upon individual autonomy was so strong as to forbid any but an ad hoc treatment of intersubjectivity. When, in addition, Sartre commits himself to the belief that dialectical transitions are *both* individually certifiable and have an aspect of necessity, he has proposed a task before which even the most resolute mind must hesitate. Unless the notion of reciprocity holds, Sartre's efforts to combine his earlier work with his social philosophy must be understood as those whose views we oppose understand him, namely, as having produced two "parts" which are much too different to be stages in a developing position.

To assess Sartre's efforts, we shall focus upon his discussion of chess as a convenient vehicle through which we can recapitulate the claims made thus far and extend them. Chess, Sartre tells us, is a "simplified symbol of actual life" in which one can see in miniature the essentials of structures like reciprocity.[1] For instance, one learns from our previous discussion of individual *praxis* that dialectical reason may be examined by considering the situation of an "abstract" individual, an organism in a field of *rareté*. The organism has needs and, because it is an internally organized unity of externally related elements, it seeks satisfaction of those needs in the surrounding material environment, the domain of externality. The penalty that it pays is to increase its object-being and thus to expose itself to danger. Sartre tells us that the penalty for the manipulation of the Other is to manipulate one's self and to become amenable to manipulation from the Other. Thus, in chess one moves in order to provoke responses from the opponent which may be used against him, but in so doing one exposes himself to a similar surpassing. Once again Sartre notes that this surpassing dif-

118

fers from that of wholly individual effort since what is surpassed is a *praxis-sujet*, not an inert entity which is not me or is the past which I slowly become. Further similarities may be seen between chess and action in the lived world; for instance, one player acts upon the other through the medium of materiality, a medium which is an essential aspect of a relationship of reciprocity. There are those who would find this claim dubious and would say that the action is wholly upon his pieces and not upon him, just as some say that a philosophical position may be attacked without attacking the person who holds it. This objection seems most unlikely in both cases if we remember how often those under attack reply so vigorously that it is clear that they do not firmly distinguish between themselves and their position. Perhaps this is nothing more than so-called "ego involvement." A Sartrean might well accept that reading because the ego for Sartre is indeed in the world, or—better—when one makes himself to be an object, at least part of what one is is that very object, thus an attack upon "it" is inevitably an attack upon the person. Whether it be writing, playing chess, or doing philosophy, the agent is exposed to a variety of perils for no other reason than the fact that he has made himself such that he can achieve purchase in the public domain, in the realm of exteriority.

If these similarities are obvious, there is one equally obvious difference between chess as an activity of externalization and the activity of the abstract individual, as obvious as the one mentioned just above. Sartre calls his example "théorique et plus simple" because the *champ pratique* in chess is much more rigorous, much more definite than the fields in which men usually find themselves involved. In principle, the number of possible moves of the pieces is calculable; in principle, a chess machine could be built which would never do less than draw. It is this feature of the field which permits the construction of chess *problems*. This feature of chess is so apparent that I have

119

a friend whom I can defeat ninety per cent of the time when there is a large number of pieces on the board but who defeats me just as regularly if we "trade off." If winning per se were the whole point to chess, his strategy ought to be to trade furiously so that the number of pieces on the board will be small enough so that the game could be "counted out," in which case I will almost certainly be counted out. It is seldom that one finds one's self in a life situation in which the field of endeavor is so neatly structured. We can think of people who conduct a great part of their lives *as if* they were so structured but surely they do so only by minute to minute maintenance of this structure, by creating "habits" or acquiring prejudices. In popularized psychological jargon, we say they are "rigid," and we say so in a tone of disapproval.

In this respect, the case of chess is not so different. A rigid situation has been created as the very locus of the game. In one case, as in the other, it is possible to achieve steadily increasing mastery of the consequences of this literal framework, and that is a task of no little difficulty. To know thoroughly the variations upon a Sicilian defense is a considerable intellectual accomplishment. To know thoroughly the "standard" openings and replies is an awesome task. Throw in a mastery of the end game and one may well have a lifetime's work before him. It would be hard to find a chess master who did not have a thorough grasp of these matters. But it would be equally hard to find a master who had *only* or even *primarily* this kind of grasp. To put the point in Sartrean terms, it would be hard to find a master who had externalized himself but had not internalized the externalization. The beginner in chess quickly learns that he must master some of the openings and at least some general principles of strategy or he cannot even provide competition for a journeyman. But he will be dismayed when he discovers that, having achieved a limited command of his skills, he will nonetheless lose frequently to one who has once commanded them but now cannot explicitly exhibit that command. At least as many apprentices drop out of chess at this point as do students of philosophy at the level of the master's degree.

The ideal combination of these factors is as trivial as it is obvious. To aspire even to competence in chess is to *seek* to combine a grasp of the mechanics with a kind of apprehension of the board which might well be called comprehension. It is all too tempting to compare the contrast between comprehension and mechanical facility to the contrast between dialectical and analytical reason. But another point must be developed first. It was said above that the *champ pratique* in chess is so definite that one could build a machine which would never do worse than draw. Even if the bulk and cost of such a machine were not prohibitive, what one wants to say is that the machine *should* not be built. Why not? For one thing, the game would no longer be chess, for the indefinite component would be eliminated. But that seems odd. When so many excellent chess players strive for just the kind of grasp the machine would display, it seems peculiar to refuse ultimate achievement. It is as though the protestor opts for obfuscation, opts for the continuance of a situation which contains as an essential ingredient his inability to do anything more than to approximate this definite apprehension. This would seem to be an aesthetic response on a par with the view that it is not winning as such which is the point to chess, but winning with a certain style. It is one thing, a mechanical thing, to be able to demonstrate mate, but it is another to show a "hopeless" position. Both fall short of actually accomplishing the mate, and there are stubborn players who insist that mate actually be achieved before they will resign. Perhaps they feel that in the further development of the position an arrangement will occur *which neither player can now envisage* which will allow them to recoup. Perhaps they feel that there is always the possibility of error on the part of the opponent, even of an error which is simply a slip of the

121

mind. It is interesting to note that there are standard responses to both of these suppositions, and the responses are significantly different. To the first, one can only say that if it is a hope for which no specific reason can be given, it cannot be eliminated but it is difficult to take seriously. This hope seems similar to what has been called "metaphysical doubt" or to have the status of a possibility which is merely logical. It is not eliminable, but nothing of additional interest follows from it. The player faced with such a cantankerous opponent will shrug wearily and go on with the game. In the second case, resentment is the usual move. If the stronger player has demonstrated his ability to play the game without trivial error by holding the very position he has achieved, to suggest that he will commit an error of this kind during the rest of the play seems tantamount to charging him with stupidity. But this is not all. Should he in fact make a foolish error, the opponent who profits from it is expected to feel chagrined, to feel that chance has entered into the game to an extent which it should not. In informal play, the opponent may even insist that the move be erased and play be begun again. One feels that it is better to have lost than to have won because of a slip of the mind or hand.

There are those who say that the attitudes discussed immediately above are "aesthetic" in the sense that reduces all too readily to a report of idiosyncratic feelings. That seems unlikely. To show this implausibility, consider that we have three distinct cases under discussion; where mate is actually consummated, where mate is demonstrated, and where it is claimed that a position is "hopeless." What the first two cases have in common is that they are both definite, both calculable. One difference between them is that the first is an accomplished fact but the second can become that only if one of the sequences is carried out without error, that is, without the kind of error which Alfred North Whitehead said was the only kind available in logic.

Perhaps that is why logicians characteristically scream at each other, for ignorance may be forgivable but stupidity is not. Note that only where a proceeding can be made wholly *definite* can stupidity be discerned. Where the domain can become wholly or largely definite, comprehension evanesces, dialectical reason is simply inappropriate. But the phrase is, "where it is *made* largely or wholly definite." My friendly opponent with the penchant for counting sometimes makes a field definite by trading off. He creates a field which *can* be calculated—by a human. But most serious chess is played at the second level, the level where mate may be demonstrated in the midst of great complexity. No doubt this is done for the sake of analytical reason itself, for surely it is more to one's credit to exhibit his facility under circumstances of great complexity than in circumstances so simple as to be trivial.

One more remark needs to be made about demonstrated mate before moving on to consider our third case, the "hopeless" position. At first we said that once the field was prepared, analytical reason could be applied. But the last comments in the preceding paragraph imply that preparation of the field is somehow an integral part of analytical reason, much as making one's self to be an object brings into being a *champ pratique* in which one may obtain object-like purchase upon that which has become another object in the field through an alien *praxis*. By reducing the number of his own pieces, and in consequence the number of mine, my calculating friend creates a field in which we both have object aspects. Then he can calculate with confidence. Consider the contrast between this situation and the "hopeless" case. What clearly distinguishes the third from the first two is the relative lack of definiteness. The players do not, and often cannot, demonstrate mate. There are several possible reasons for that. With beginners, it may be sheer ignorance. They just do not see how they can proceed toward anything like mate and they mistake their ignorance for a trait of the board. Frequently, this means that they do not see how they could get to the point of demonstrating. For a veteran, the situation is quite different. On the one hand, he may know from experience that a situation in which he has been forced to trade a rook for a knight will almost surely be disastrous in the end. This kind of understanding is very close to that required by demonstration. But he may also say something like, "I just don't like this position," without being able to specify just what structures of the game portend disaster. In both of these varieties of the claim that a position is hopeless, the chance of being mistaken is much greater than in the case of demonstration. Both players assume that the one who makes the judgment is a master of the mechanics of the game but has so interiorized them that he no longer *explicitly* makes use of them although, like the demonstrator, he may always make the stupid mistakes which are available. Like the scientist who can't tell you just how he derived an hypothesis, but who has considerable success with his "hunches," the expert in chess will seldom be able to further specify his grasp. Like the scientist, he, too, has a test. He can play out the game. But when he is done, it will not always be possible to look back and show *definitely* how the final position resulted from the position he had called hopeless. Not even the continuing record kept of the game will accomplish this specification for *all it tells you is what moves have in fact been made.* It will not tell you, for instance, that on move number seven, the knight was used instead of the bishop because the player happens to have a fondness for knights, a fondness for their inherent duplicity in contrast to the relatively straightforward attitude of the bishop.

No *determinate* account of the game will reveal the "hopeless" character of the position precisely because the position in this case is not the place of the pieces on the board, nor is it these plus the possible combinations and permutations to which they lend themselves. The position here includes these factors, these definite elements, but it *also* includes both players. "If I go there, he can go there. Will he? Of course he will. No other course of action is as promising. Would I if I were he? I don't know. I wouldn't if I saw that masked check. But he prefers bold play and may want to run the risk to gain control at K5." We need not continue. Because our opponent—and ourselves—are *parts* of the field, we must consider his possibilities as much as we consider those of the pieces. But the process of consideration is quite different. The pieces are only objects. He is a subject-object. One can try to emphasize his object aspect so that his subjectivity becomes irrelevant. To succeed in this attempt would be to create a situation in which *demonstration* is possible. But a quite different course is also available. To make the claim to a hopeless position is to endorse the subjectivity of the Other, to accord to him an irreducible level of subjectivity, to accord to him the honor of being taken as fully human. It is also to insist upon one's own humanity, but not merely in the sense that one might be in error. In the argot of the contemporary academic community, to be "human" appears to be to make mistakes, to pretend that one does not, and to admit one's fallibility and deviousness with much show of humility. That is the kind of attitude one might take with respect to the first of the cases we have discussed. But the claim to a hopeless position, or the acceptance of that claim, is not "human" in this sense. Far from a display of humility—false or not—it displays an almost Nietzschean arrogance, for it is available only among equals, that is, subjectivities presumed to be resourceful—to use a Sartrean phrase, "men in possession of their own destinies."

It is not at all clear from Sartre's discussion of chess that he understands these aspects of the third case. He understands that the combat is one in which subjectivities struggle to transcend each other's transcendence through their object-being, but it is not clear that he understands how one might cease the struggle out of *respect* for a resourceful opponent and out of respect for one's own resources. One wonders whether he would understand that it is from a parallel "style" that we say that the chess machine *should* not be built. But he understands very well that this realm of struggle, however concluded, is the realm of a nondeterminate. The "reasoning" is done in what has been called a domain of ambiguity, what Merleau-Ponty called the world of probability, and, perhaps, the realm which Anglo-Saxon philosophers call that of "ordinary English." It must be immediately noted that this arena is by no means the place of cognitive or perceptual rhapsody. There are "structures" in it. There are definite elements. Only knights can jump other pieces. The possession of two rooks in the end game is a near guarantee of victory over the possessor of two bishops. The possession of tempo creates the likelihood of victory. But the field *also* contains an essential ingredient of indefiniteness, not only as a margin, but as integral to the domain. To be alert to the possibility of a claim to a hopeless position is to attempt to operate with ambiguity as such. To do so is as difficult as it is dangerous. Failure to attend explicitly to the definite structures of the field can lead to disaster even where one has mastered the techniques. To suggest a parallel circumstance, metaphysicians do sometimes commit merely logical errors. But the temptation to what some call "cracker barrel philosophy" is even more dangerous. Because the ordinary life world has the same texture as the world of the dialectician or the consummate chess player, the assertions made by the dialectician are also made by the most callow beginner, and some of the evidence offered is the same. We suggest that it is this similar texture which accounts for the situation so familiar to the academic philosopher, where he is seldom an authority on any other subject, but everyone is an authority in philosophy. Sartre's claim that dialectical necessity is always a necessity *for* someone can easily be confused with the quite different

126

claim that something is "true for me." For one who is only externally acquainted with the literature of existentialism, it is often very difficult to tell whether he is faced with the country store variety of philosophy or with the professional type. This is particularly true of professional philosophers of another persuasion. At the same time, the ready availability of either reading is one of the central reasons for the vogue which various versions of existentialism have enjoyed. The paradox is delightful.

The paradox is also frustrating to one who has attempted to internalize the dialectic. One wants to say that some have come to the "right" conclusions for the "wrong" reasons just as a chess veteran might say that a beginner has put him in a hopeless position even though the beginner did not know what he was doing. This frustration is deepened by the dialectician's realization that the similarity in the texture of the ordinary life world and his own realm may lead him to deceive himself. While in the grip of an idea which is taking shape easily on a typewriter, the writer has no doubt about the plausibility or even of the truth of what he is saying. But all too often a reading of what has been written gives quite a different impression, an impression like that gained by a philosopher of some other persuasion who reads the in-group literature of phenomenology and existentialism. We sometimes discover that we are doing cracker barrel philosophy when we thought during the process that it was dialectical. Sometimes chess is played with sensitivity, and sometimes the play is just plain sloppy. Too often this is discovered only when the position is hopeless. It is painful to discover that what we say and write deceives others, but it is excruciating to discover self-deception.

Nonetheless, the risk must be taken unless the choice is to be restricted to actual accomplishment or to demonstration. In Sartrean terms, the philosopher must try to cope with ambiguity in its own terms unless he is willing to restrict himself to the

127

domain and the procedures of analytical reason. The phenomenologists are quite right in saying that ambiguity is inescapable even if a commitment of definiteness is made. This is so because of the presence of the margin, and because the penalty for definiteness is the suppression or neglect of some indefinite elements, even where the elements rejected are consigned to the limbo of appearance. But—again—there is a variety of choices as to how one shall deal with ambiguity. One method has already been indicated. The indefinite is simply neglected, exiled. Another response to ambiguity would be that so often attributed to the mystic. One "quiets the mind" and speaks, if at all, in parables. Sartre opts for a third alternative which is to attempt a synthetic union of paradox and system. Witness on the one hand the familiar formula, "Man makes history precisely insofar as history makes man," and on the other hand the deliberate architectonic of the tome from which that epigram is taken. The chess master can do no less. He must be able to calculate and must sometimes actually do so. End games played intuitively are rarely successful. But, if the account given here of the master's game is correct, he must also be able to deal with the board where calculation is impractical or impossible. What is suggested here is that the dialectician is in a situation much like that of the chess master and that *CRD* is the work of a consummate player.

But the parallel must not be pressed too far, for there is at least one major difference between chess and the ordinary life world which casts doubt upon this correlation whether that world be dealt with by ordinary means or by explicit recourse to dialectical reason. Chess begins with a domain made wholly definite, a realm which in principle can be counted out. Remember the chess machine. The life world apparently lacks this feature unless it be supposed that there is a reality of a definite kind "behind the appearances." That many philosophers have so supposed is patent, but there is also reason to do so in

128

quite ordinary experience. I am almost completely ignorant of the mechanical composition of my automobile. I deal with it wholly through "appearances." I shift when the motor hits a certain pitch. I notice if the gears are mushy. I note that it whines in second. Fortunately, the mechanic at the service station not only has this sort of information but he also knows the machine as a machine, and when he performs operations upon it he frequently changes the phenomena in terms of which I relate to the machine. Here there is a reality behind the appearances, even though it remains opaque to me despite the patient explanations with which the mechanic occasionally indulges me. I do indeed "live" that car, but, for *at least certain purposes*, I should be the last to say that my grasp was more fundamental than that which the mechanic has. It may be that I have the "feel" of my car in a way that he does not and that I would thus note things which would not turn up on the semiannual inspection, but when what I note is *also* unacceptable my presumed advantage all but disappears. Similar comments could be made about my body with respect to my view and a physician's, but the point is sufficiently illustrated. Not only *may* there be a reality behind the appearances, not only may the arguments of those philosophers who support such a view be triumphant, but there is reason in our ordinary dealings with the life world to entertain this thesis. This feature was only apparently lacking from the life world. The parallel to chess, it seems, should be reinstated.

But one has the feeling that the comments immediately above are too gross, too enthusiastically put, and too hastily accepted. Like my automobile, chess has an underlying structure which is both physical and calculable. Unlike the case with my car, I know the structure and can manipulate it in the way in which the mechanic manipulates my car. On many occasions the "lived" character of the game is due to my failure to manipulate correctly. I have even been known to miscalculate the

129

position resulting from a pawn *en passent*. In chess, I am both driver and mechanic. But the influence of the structure of the game is even more pervasive than that. Chinese chess is sufficiently similar to chess to allow one to play the Oriental game badly after a minimum of instruction, but the fact that a "cannon" can jump pieces while still performing the functions of a rook makes a very great difference between the texture of the two games. No claim is made here that the differences are all so directly related to the physical limitations. Only some vital features are thus related, related in a manner which requires a "comprehension" which is almost of a different species. Fords and Jaguars are much more alike than chess and Chinese chess. Nevertheless, it makes more sense to say of an engine that it is one thing and that my grasp of it is another than it does to say the same of the board and my grasp of it in chess. To be fair, of course, I should have compared *driving* an automobile to *playing* chess. But notice that I might have said "to compare driving an automobile to chess" without using the verb "playing" to emphasize action or process. There are chess sets and automobiles, and there are people who play chess and people who drive automobiles, and there is chess and—what? The breakdown of the parallel suggests the kind of difference which is in point. The physical structure of chess is much more an integral part of the game itself than the automobile is of driving. Notice that I had to use the participle again. To put the point another way, the distinction between object and subject is much greater in driving than it is in chess. Perhaps that is because— as Sartre says—part of chess is making another subject-object to be an object-subject. But our intent at the moment is only to indicate the phenomenon, not to offer an explanation.

Our interest in presenting the phenomenon is in order to treat automobiles and chess as members of a series in an increasing order of nondeterminateness, or, if you prefer, of ambiguity. But a further point first. Both the automotive realm and the

130

chess world have the definiteness they have due to human decision, to human action. Both involve *matière ouvrée*. Men bring these objects into being and maintain them in being in order to accomplish various goals. Men make themselves to be objects and in so doing carve out a *champ pratique*. Both instrumentalities are to be surpassed although there are those who are reluctant in both cases to go beyond the merely mechanical. Some people want to work chess down to the point of calculation and some people insist on automatic transmissions. But please note that, of those who drive, many more would welcome further definiteness than would those who play chess. Drivers would welcome automatic pilots and look forward with anticipation to the time when super highways have guidance tracks like those on slot tracks. Chess players, we claim, would not want the chess machine to be built. The purpose of automobiles is to get from one place to another with *maximum efficiency*. If that goal demands a minimization of the driver's activities, it is nonetheless driving. Indeed, it is better. But if chess were similarly made efficient not only would it be worse, it would not be chess at all. The physical framework of the game is constructed *in order to be surpassed*, that is, both annulled and preserved. It must somehow be maintained from game to game and yet be incorporated differently in each game or at least in each kind of game. The player who *seeks* to return to the mechanical level, even to that of demonstration, simply does not *comprehend* the game.

Driving and chess, then, occupy two distinguishable levels in the series of increasing order of nondefiniteness which I am attempting to construct. There are at least two more levels to be mentioned. The first of these—the third, overall—is that which we called the "ordinary" way of dealing with the life world, providing we except the case of automobiles in the way in which I have used it. Let us use the exception to characterize the rule. My grasp of the operation of an automobile is very little different from that of my life. My grasp of mechanical contrivances in general is very much like that of the stereotype of the "helpless female." But one notices rather quickly that some women—faculty wives, for instance—who have the misfortune to be married to mechanical idiots soon become adept at minor repairs. This indicates that the need for a "man around the house" stems less from incapacity than from refusal. No doubt the same is true of men with respect to the need for a cook and housekeeper—and when my wife reads *that* line, I'm in big trouble! Much as one can *choose* to deal with a car or a chess game mechanically, one can also *refuse* to do so. In Sartre's view, one cannot in general refuse to become an object, but that belief is not incompatible with the claims presented here. Such refusal is even more obvious when it is other *people* with whom one is dealing. Although I suspect this is mere folk-wisdom, the legendary insistence of women upon dealing "emotionally" with others rather than dealing with them in a fashion which men call "rational" is a massive example of the refusal to commit oneself wholeheartedly to externality. Sartre's famous description of emotion as a "magical" change of an aspect of the life world which one cannot change in reality is in point here. But, if it is agreed that the life world consists chiefly of relations to others through the medium of a material upon which man has set his seal, that is, if it is agreed that *reciprocity* is the most fundamental of human relations, then the refusal to make the structural an end in itself is the most characteristic mark of this domain. Human relations which are minimally institutionalized form this third level of the non-definite in which not only is there a greater degree of indefiniteness but in which men *insist* upon maintaining that degree of inherence.

But surely I have overstated the point. It is Sartre who claims that individual *praxis* necessarily produces the antidialectic. Some forms of alienation are functions of contingent circum-

132

stances. Even those oppressive structures resulting from *praxis* on the basis of scarcity are functions of this kind since it is at least possible that scarcity is not the domain of every conceivable stage of human development but only the background of what human development has been thus far. But alienation itself is not accidental any more than the need to externalize one's self is accidental. The "abstract" individual, the human organism, is an internal unity of *externally* related elements. The institutions which men create to enhance their humanity inevitably become the instruments of their dehumanization. The *groupe en fusion* becomes group, the group becomes institution, the institution becomes bureaucratic. Prophets on all sides tell us that human beings are increasingly likely to become their functions, and the creatures of Huxley's imagination threaten to materialize as have Buck Rogers and his crew. The "tone" of *CRD* certainly reflects the inert to a much greater extent than did *Being and Nothingness*. Once one passes the stage of the *groupe en fusion*, ossification sets in. But nowhere does Sartre assert that one should—much less that one must—acquiesce in this progressive objectification. *CRD* is itself an exhaustive—and exhausting—attempt to combat the sclerosis which has overtaken Marxism in its neo-Stalinist form. Even if human effort necessarily ends in the inert, it may always begin again, for neither collectives nor groups nor institutions have any support more fundamental than individual *praxis* even if that *praxis* be directed toward its own minimization as in tyrannies of either the Left or the Right. It is true that the individual human is much more subject to exploitation than the "common" individual, and it is true that, for Sartre, man is most human in the group "correctly" managed or, since groups are seldom if ever properly managed, in the *groupe en fusion*. But since there is *in fact* no abstract individual—except as the limit of social organization—the social groupings Sartre endorses are preferred because it is in them that human action

133

is closest to individual *praxis*, farthest from the definite forms which are characteristic of tyranny. It is in the group correctly managed that men achieve the most efficient form of an organization which still remains *human*. Beyond that, the penalty for further efficiency is dehumanization. In fairness one must say that as the scope of human effort increases, definiteness becomes more compelling so that dehumanization is not directly chosen by the apostles of efficiency. A small college can tolerate ambiguity much more easily than a large university. But notice that the word is "can" tolerate. Not all do what they can. But the closer we get to individual effort, the more obvious it is that we *choose* to accept, extend, or limit the definiteness which is permitted in the world. It is not at all obvious that sentences of the type, "Human beings cannot be dealt with by the methods of natural science," are claims. They may well be expressions of insistence, expressions of refusal.

But now I have trapped myself, for chess is above all things a matter of individual human effort and I have called reciprocal action most human, least definite when it approaches the level of individual effort. Yet I have called that level a stage of greater indefiniteness than the stage at which I located chess. There are two responses to this presumed difficulty. First, chess is treated by Sartre as a situation deliberately arranged so that the reciprocity involved is *antagonistique*. Each player tries to make of the other a "surpassing-surpassed." Although all human relations include an element of negativity, not all are antagonistic, or at least not in the institutionalized fashion of chess. Chess, after all, is a *game*, perhaps even a contest. Chess is at the upper limit of the range of nondefiniteness just below that of individual *praxis*. Chess is hardly an ordinary human activity. Since the members of the series which is being constructed here are distinct but not mutually exclusive, the ingredient of individuality involved in chess is simply the reflection of the absence of strict boundaries. Second, and more impor-

134

tant, chess includes a field which is more definite than that available in any ordinary human activity. The board and the rules are *given* and one cannot deviate from them and still play the game. While there are rules and procedures in most human activity, they are for the most part less definite than those of chess both in their statement and in the range of permissible interpretation. The difference can be seen most easily by reflecting upon the fact that most human activities include an explicit provision for the excuse of error. The only place this element has in chess is the case mentioned earlier where one sometimes allows an opponent to take back a move. But even this is strictly illegal and one offers the opportunity with hesitation and accepts it with chagrin. One can fudge about coming to a full stop at an intersection knowing full well that he can be arrested for it but probably will not be, but one cannot fudge the move of the bishop so that it becomes slightly rectangular. If philosophical analysis has taught us anything in the last thirty years, it has taught us that the domain expressed through ordinary English is not explicitly structured but is a realm of shadings and nuance where there are no rules if there are no procedures. But to say this is to say that the structure of the ordinary life world is sufficiently indefinite to require explicit action in order to develop rules from procedures. There is nothing there which is comparable to the board, the pieces, and the rules of manipulation in chess. This is not to deny that the life world may be *made to be* more definite. Some of the Orwellian pangs suffered by contemporary writers witness the all too ready availability of definite construction. But—again—it *may* be thus treated. It need not be, and the penalties for ignoring what definiteness it does have are not as great as they are for ignoring the proper moves of the pieces in chess. Not only is there more "room" to remain in the realm of ambiguity but the penalty for doing so is less. It is no wonder that humans ordinarily *insist* that ambiguity be maintained, that their feelings be respected, their idiosyncracies be indulged, and their games involve a notable element of chance.

Once again I have exaggerated, and that exaggeration requires a certain modification. There are some elements of definiteness in the ordinary domain; otherwise it could not be treated as if it were pervasively structured. Part of what is meant by calling science the "long arm of common sense" is that the factor of definiteness is stressed through the ulitization of techniques amenable to mathematical interpretation and through restricting attention to only one type of direct involvement in the world, the type we call sense perception. From this point of view, to suppose that science discovers a reality behind the appearances or to take claims about the domain of scientific objects and make them the ground for the denial of the deliverances of lived experience, is simply hilarious. One can assign whatever index of objectivity one wishes to science by treating it as the study of the definite structures of the nondefinite as they are exhibited through sense perception under the tutelage of mathematics. If there are those who come to insist upon living the totality of their experiences through the attitude and the methods of this kind of making-definite, that is their business, but, if there is any ground of "objective" truth, it surely is not insistence. The vogue of science in our time is not only a function of its magnificent successes, nor of the challenge it offers to strenuous efforts by capable minds, but is also due to the fact that it is *one* natural result of continued emphasis upon making one's world definite in a way which is familiar to everyman. There is no intent here to damn science with faint praise or to suggest that it is somehow inferior to another kind of *praxis* which would be less enamored of the specifiable. From our point of view, philosophy itself—or at least traditional philosophy—is the result of the same emphasis. So, too, religion as any prophet shows us when he raises his voice against the priests. For a Sartrean, there is no court of appeal

136

beyond one's foundational choice of being, however difficult it may be to bear the idiosyncracies of one's fellows.

But what of the dialectician? And what of Sartre? It was suggested earlier that he was at the highest level of nondefiniteness among those levels which have been considered. Does this mean that he must be utterly contemptuous of definiteness? Not at all. Chess played at the third level does not *exclude* definiteness; it surpasses its earlier forms. No human action begins in a wholly unstructured field whether that action be the awakening to one's "situation," the implementation of revolution, or the writing of a lengthy treatise on *la Raison dialectique*. For Sartre, there is no such thing as nonsituated knowing. Since dialectic is knowing par excellence, structure is unavoidable. But the reduction of the realm to its structures is not the end to be achieved. To win is not the only end in chess played well and is not the most fundamental goal sought. Sartre tells us that he seeks to exhibit a grasp of history from within which will be sure, but that this grasp, even if achieved, will not be wholly definite and *thus* not "publicly" certified although it will be available to those who are willing and able to seek. To assess Sartre's conclusions concerning dialectical reason requires that one work one's way through *CRD* with the same seriousness with which it was written. To assess the claim that there is a grasp of chess at the third level requires that one work one's way through stages one and two. There are some claims that can be evaluated only by going through the process from which they allegedly arise whether that process consist in internalizing seven hundred contorted pages or whether it involves several years of chess. In either case, it is obvious that the element of definiteness is not only unavoidable but is necessary to the achievement of a non-definite grasp. As Sartre has always said, resistance is the necessary correlate of effort. What he has said here is that struggle is a necessary condition of comprehension. But comprehension is the name of precisely that grasp which is required of the dialectician and available only to him. From the standpoint of adherents of the definite, comprehension is mere mystification. From the standpoint of the purveyors of the indefinite, the "theistic" existentialists, comprehension is a barrier to the achievement of rational non-knowledge. Sartre's point is that comprehension is the only mode of access to the Other which is bilateral, which not only respects but insists upon mutual autonomy. But that is to say that comprehension is the noetic correlate of reciprocity. Note that, as different as they are, those who advocate the definite and those who advocate the indefinite have a striking commonality. The mode in which they advance their position is unilateral. The habitual proceeding of the devotee of the indefinite is instruction. Being possessed of the truth, he informs the uninitiated, or, if the uninitiated are also untutored, he leads them to the threshold of discovery through persuasion. The advocate of definiteness also instructs, but, like the world he lives, his instruction is less likely to be persuasive than it is to be coercive. In his case, as in the case of his apparent opposite, the Other is treated as an event to be moulded into the "correct" form. The methods of Mayor Daley's police and those of the "peaceful" demonstrators are significantly different, but neither can be viewed as stemming from a profound acknowledgement of the autonomy of the other. It is precisely this autonomy which comprehension, dialectic, and reciprocity insist upon. In chess, if one encounters another who is not one's equal, the preferred mode of response is to refrain from the use of techniques which are clearly beyond his grasp. *Chess is a game which is most fully itself only when played by equals.* Because it is, it is a paradigm case for the display of the essentials of the idea of reciprocity. In it, as in dialectic, only men who are fully human can play well. In the world of which dialectic is both the method and the content, autonomy and relatedness, particularity and generality, are not only desirable but inescapable. But if this is so, re-

138

ciprocity is as fundamental and omnipresent as Sartre has claimed it is—and so is that free being whom Sartre has so long championed.

Six

THE VARIETIES
OF REASON
IN *CRD*

It is clear that Sartre is no more willing to sacrifice comprehension to persuasion or to instruction than he is to sacrifice autonomy to mutual dependence. Chess is by no means as definite as checkers, but neither inspiration nor insight alone is a sufficient condition for success in the King's game. At the same time, the mere mastery of patterns is no less inadequate. From Plato's vision of the Good to Karl Jaspers' thrust beyond shipwreck, a continuing philosophical tradition endorses the belief that only the person who masters the rules may speak of what is beyond the domain of definite structure. Sartre is no stranger to that tradition. Neither is he wholly in accord with it, for his advocacy of autonomy leads him to emphasize commitment, that "choice" which, because it is in fact or in effect a choice of rules, is itself not a product of rules, not even an emergent product. What this means is that Sartre's insistence upon the fundamentality of reciprocity with its constituent autonomy is the reflection in his later thought of the freedom of the individual which he has always insisted upon. If we extend our discussion of chess to gaming in general, we can readily see an analogy between this controversial element in Sartre's thought and an ingredient in any activity which we ordinarily call a game. Many of those activities involve an element of sheer invention. Even if we wish to say that the rules of the game are simply the result of decisions to standardize existing procedures, the standardization itself is certainly the result of a choice from among several possible alternatives. If one notices the centrality of the concept of a rule in any activity which we are likely to call a game, it is easy to say that the game has been invented. Entirely apart from the merits of this inference, there are, in fact, games which are invented, for instance, those which young children constantly concoct for their own amusement and those which adults invent in order to exercise their capacities. What is suggested here is that the concept of commitment in Sartre's thought bears a structural analogy to the concept of invention in gaming. Similarly, the idea that games are invented bears an enticing affinity to Sartre's claim that the necessity sometimes attributed to games like symbolic logic is simply a specification of the necessity which dialectical reason imparts to the framework of definite games, that is, to analytical reason. Should commitment turn out to be as essential to a human life being human as invention is to a game being a game, then we shall see that in this, the last of our lengthy encounters with these familiar notions, Sartre's Marxism is just the latest of his encounters with the notion of the human reality as freedom in a situation.

To consider commitment in the context of gaming in general, we should begin by focusing upon the more familiar notion of "choice." I can, for instance, choose to engage in activities which go on in the realm of what Sartre calls analytical reason. For purposes of teaching elementary deductive logic, I can choose to correlate if-then statements in English with the

142

material conditional so that my system will be elegant, so that my decision procedure will be effective. I can choose to consider all administrators as mortal enemies whose actions are predictable over time although elusive in detail. I can commit myself to a "behaviorist" stance without making any assertion about its superiority over the black magic of psychoanalysis. One commonality stands out from these examples. The expression "I can choose" or "I can commit myself" indicates through its repetition that I am free to do otherwise. It takes very little to transmute this reading into a version of the standard game metaphor. I need not make myself to be an object unless I choose to type effectively. If I wish to be understood as "hard nosed," I can choose to become an experimentalist, but clearly I need not seek to elicit that appraisal from the Other. I can choose to commit myself to analytical reason or to the dialectical variety of reason. I can conceivably decide to do this for reasons as demeaning as the desire to maximize the opportunity to get a job on one side of the English Channel rather than on the other. This "game" reading is by no means inconsistent with Sartrean themes. The free being of *Being and Nothingness* was able to choose between acting for the sake of freedom or collaboration. It was even possible for a child of the petty bourgeoisie to join revolutionaries whose activities were designed to destroy the source of much of his well being, including the money he used to attend a school where he could becomes a revolutionary. The lonely individual could choose his own game were he only willing to accept the consequences. Being, Sartre said, is contingently necessary but it is also necessarily contingent.

But objections to the above arise even as one reads it. For instance, the very language in which the choices of the man who is his freedom are described makes one uneasy about thinking of this as a game. Activities in the life world can scarcely be described by terms which bear such frivolous connotations.

Real choices are serious, anguished, compelling. Would you believe "existential"? The objection itself is not serious. There are games which are no less compelling than any other "life form." Abundant evidence for that claim will be supplied by many a faculty wife who has seen her husband turn into a monster over the bridge table. Where the term "existential" means "impassioned" or "involved"—and too often it means little more than that—nothing prevents the application of the game metaphor to situations which are the stock in trade of the existential novel. A stronger objection may be offered by directing one's attention to an apparent play upon the ambiguity of the term "choice." While I may choose to sit down and play a hand of bridge, it seems odd to say that I might choose collaboration. For one thing, I should expect to find myself already collaborating so that my option would be to continue to do what I'm doing rather than to begin to do so. For another, to say that the choice of collaboration is to be understood as a manifestation of an original choice of being is somehow much more plausible than to say that a commitment to bridge reflects some such fundamental orientation. But the most interesting issue which emerges from these reflections is that the original choice of being is "choice" in what must seem to most a Pickwickean sense. The chief burden of the English term "choice" is a decision among options based upon deliberation and in that sense "rational." *If* I can say that I find that I have chosen, this deliberated entertainment of options and evidence seems unlikely. Consider, for example, A. I. Melden's discussion of action in which he suggests that we internalize the rules according to which we act although neither the process of acculturation nor the specific decisions taken upon that basis are the result of conscious deliberation. There is an even more radical aspect to the Sartrean sense of "choice," the aspect that has led some to distinguish it from the deliberative sense by calling it "commitment." It would be strange indeed to speak of the "original choice of being" as the sort of thing one does when he learns proper social behavior or the proper use of moral terms. It would be equally strange to speak of the choice of collaboration or of anti-Semitism as one speaks of the internalization of rules, even though neither of those orientations seems as impressive as an original choice of being. In any case, it seems inappropriate to apply the game metaphor to the choice between analytical and dialectical reason whether one emphasizes the contingency of the decision to play or whether one emphasizes the manner in which one learns to play.

We say "seems inappropriate" because the suspicion lingers that while this second objection is not *merely* a statement of an attitude as was the first objection, an attitudinal element of no little strength is nonetheless involved. To the extent that it is, one may simply accept or reject the objection without analysis or argument. Rather than debate the appropriateness of this abrupt response to the second of these familiar but insubstantial objections, we should seek for those which minimize the attitudinal element. Reflect, if you will, upon the claim that one can choose analytical reason as one might choose to become an experimental psychologist. Once again one commits himself to procedures which create a region in which analytical techniques have efficacy. One chooses to deal with phenomena which are publicly observable by applying known experimental methods and by a mode of thought highly structured by its mathematical component. To vary the illustration, recall our earlier discussion of a man who chooses to engage in geometry, that is, who chooses to limit his attention to relations in a field of externality, to the *sillage* of a synthetic process. Reasons could be offered for the choice of experimental instead of clinical psychology, thus the choice would not appear to be a commitment. But notice that the very offering of reasons indicates that the fact of choice itself was not part and parcel of the game chosen. Thus, it is of interest to ask whether the fact of choice

145

is itself part of any game. Clearly it is not. The notion of game used here includes an essential reference to a non-game activity in a non-game domain. To say that I have chosen to play some game is to say that there was at least one other alternative. But suppose the alternative was itself another game? Then my choice is between one of two types of games and there is still another alternative, namely, that which is other than a game, that which is required as the contrast in terms of which it is meaningful to speak of a game. If it is not meaningful to speak of "false" apart from "true" or of "appearance" apart from "reality," it is not meaningful to speak of a game apart from its proper contrary. One might well expect the same to be the case with respect to analytical reason and its apparent contrary. But dialectical reason is not a contrary in the same sense, for if it is *that within which* analytical reason is merely a moment, the analogy to the non-game area is incomplete.

But the analogy is not entirely without value because it calls attention to Sartrean views which also lead to the rejection of the game metaphor. While it makes some sense to speak of choosing a particular activity or of making oneself to be an object of a certain kind in order to obtain the leverage required to satisfy some need, it makes little sense to speak of choosing in general to become an object. One does not choose to be in need. One no more chooses to be a lack than one chooses to be nothingness or chooses to be a freedom. As we saw in Sartre's discussion of individual *praxis*, the organism in need is an integral part of the field of externally related elements even though it is an internally organized unity of them. This description of an organism is by no means Sartre's clearest. The lack which is lived as need by the organism can and sometimes must be remedied by a mere addition or subtraction of externally related elements, a circumstance which makes one wonder about the claim that the internal organization of the organism is as crucial to its being-as-organism as Sartre would have us think.

146

Perhaps all one can say is that, for Sartre, the occurrence of organisms is given, and, because he will not argue, much less abandon, that belief, he tolerates puzzles. But one might also say that Sartre's individual has an object aspect integral to its very being and whatever the resultant puzzles, that, too, must be recognized. If there were no such object aspect from the "beginning," the act of making one's self to be an object would be completely unintelligible. What occurs, perhaps, is an *emphasis* upon the object aspect of the individual. But this use of "emphasis" must not suggest deliberate or even explicit awareness. One can fall into lethargy as well as deliberately withdraw. One can emphasize one's object aspect precisely because it is an essential feature of the unstable tension which one calls the human organism.

Shall we say that because the organism has an object aspect, it *must* at some time emphasize it? The most that one can apparently say is that the individual is able to emphasize because of prior possession. But part of the point to calling an organism an unstable tension is to indicate that to be an organism is to be fluctuating among various aspects. Although Sartre entertains the notion of the rhythmic persistence of a stable individual, in the world we have, in a world permeated by *rareté*, the continued self-fulfillment of an organism is continually interrupted. Scarcity is internalized as lack and lived as a further relation to the environment, need. In this world, the individual does not have the option of accepting or rejecting fluctuation. If it did, it would not be *this* kind of individual. The question is not whether we shall emphasize but of which emphasis we shall make the most, just as in the earlier Sartre, the question was not whether we shall act but which kind of action we should undertake. But now it must be added that any emphasis will give rise to its contrary, that the unstable tension is a unity of *opposites*, that dialectic is the logic of individual *praxis*, because the individual is understood best through the categories

147

of historical materialism. One must not forget that Sartre by his own claim is a Marxist even if his brethren are reluctant to acknowledge him. What we contend is that there are philosophical as well as ideological reasons for Sartre's Marxism.

While it may be plausible to compare the emphasis upon some aspect of the individual to the choice of a particular activity as a "game," the plausibility does not extend to gaming in general. The contingency which infects Being does not directly extend to an action in the field of scarcity any more than it extends directly to the free being of *Being and Nothingness*. Scarcity itself is a contingent feature of the world we now have, but, as Sartre notes repeatedly, scarcity has its inevitable consequences. Need is one of those consequences, *praxis* is another. It was Sartre's true teacher, Hegel, who said that the transition from one abstraction to its opposite was necessary for a mind able to exert the required effort and willing to pay the dialectical penalty. That idea is no less true for the student who refuses the Hegelian view that Spirit is the truth of the real in favor of the view that man is both in and conscious of the world. If it is true that Spirit must so embody itself that it is unrecognizable to itself, it is no less true that *praxis* is necessarily alienated, that it must become the antidialectic, that it will become *praxis-processus*. There are forms of alienation which can be surpassed, but alienation itself is inescapable. One does not choose to accept or to reject alienation per se. To be is to be alienated. To be is to be involved. To be is to totalize and retotalize so that one's world is never the same. One can only hope that it is a process of enrichment in at least some of its incessantly changing stages.

To be human is to totalize, or—better—to be a human organism is to be both totality and totalization. To be an organism in a field of externality is to be the continuing attempt to achieve the dynamic analogue of the completeness of being-in-itself, that is, cyclical harmony. But neither organism nor need

148

nor *praxis* are *the* fundamental set of terms in Sartre's whole position. One must remember that the free being of *Being and Nothingness* was condemned to be free. One must also remember that the desire to be God, the desire to be the stable coincidence of being, and the consciousness of being was said *to be* the human reality. Let us put it bluntly. The human reality is *necessarily* a useless passion. The organism is *necessarily* the attempt to be a dynamic totality, and the name of that attempt is totalization. Need is not a function of the structures of the field of scarcity which *happen* to be the most pervasive characteristic of the world we *happen* to have. It is the result of the intrinsic "nature" of the organism which would hold in any field whether that field featured scarcity or not. One can accept the contention that scarcity is as fundamental a determinant as *CRD* maintains only if one refuses the hallmark of contingency to which Sartre intermittently refers. If to speak of scarcity as contingent is to call attention to the contingency of being in general, all well and good. The obvious economic connotations of the term are then merely a persuasive device to allow Sartre to slip into a "Marxist" anthropology from a phenomenological ontology. But, if scarcity is to be taken as one of the forms under which contingency reveals itself in a particular epoch of history or even through the course of history thus far, then Sartre misleads us in using the term. In a realm not characterized by scarcity, an organism would still be an organism and thus be the attempt to achieve that impossible coincidence which is here called by the name "dynamic totality," a naming which is merely a device to call attention to a self-perpetuating whole composed of not wholly compatible elements. Sartre may well be a Marxist. He may well be an "historical materialist." But he is also an ontologist, and, if the world of this historical being now includes an emphasis which obscures that fact, let us unearth it and take it as seriously as he once did, and, for all one can *demonstrate*, as seriously as he still does.

The discussion just above is open to an immediate challenge: "Do you presume to attribute to Sartre the claim that organisms have a *nature*? May we now expect the absurdity of a similar move when the adjective 'human' is added?" The response is that a nature is attributed here in the same sense that one may say that Sartre posits a nature in saying that man *is* the desire to be God. The validity of the attribution will be left to the judgment of the reader. The point will be no different when "human" is added. Man "is" a material being of the organic kind which also arises as a reflection upon being. That action which is thus reflected-reflecting gives rise to collectives which are so tangible as to enable Laing to say that they are material beings. It is scarcely surprising that a plurality of material individuals should give rise to such. But it is a bit startling to realize that Sartre does not hesitate to speak of totalizations without totalizers, actions with no agent, and that he distinguishes the apprehension of phenomena like these by the term "intellection," reserving "comprehension" for situations in which present human agency is an essential factor. No one has been more outspoken than Sartre in opposing the reification of notions like class, culture, history and the like. But it could scarcely be otherwise if it is true, as Sartre claims, that relations among men are "mediated" by matter. Nor is Sartre's set contravened by noting that men are the mediation between various sectors of materiality, that man is the product of *his* product. If men may be dehumanized by matter, so matter can be, and is, humanized by men.

The point is delicate. We do not want to say that history makes men in the sense that there exists some peculiar entity called history which operates upon men externally. To speak in this fashion is to speak of distinctions as though they were separations, to speak as one so often speaks if analytic reason is taken as reason's primary variety. Similarly, one does not wish to commit the orthodox Marxist's error of projecting relationships discovered in the historical and social context to the

150

world conceived under the title of Nature and then to speak of them as forces external to individuals, forces which could only exist *for* a universal mind. On the other hand, Sartre is not content to treat collective phenomena as statistical unities, much less as constructs, or even as regulative ideas. No follower of Marx, however far removed from the paths of orthodoxy, can countenance an ontology which endorses the idea of an individual who is fully real *qua* individual. Sartre characterizes his discussion of individual *praxis* as "abstract" in the Hegelian sense. The *champ pratique* created by an individual *praxis* is ingredient in a domain similarly totalized by a plurality of agents so that it is not matter upon which man usually works but *matière ouvrée*. The field in which a human finds himself includes other humans and their objectifications as essential structures. Men work and are worked upon by other men and their works. The foundation of all further human relationships is relations which are reciprocal or triadic. If a totalization is not *reducible* to this set of fundamental elements—and it is not —it certainly is not reducible to individual *praxis* considered abstractly. Sartre does not even threaten any such reduction. The idea of the individual is the result of an analysis of a prior synthetic unity, and Sartre does not forget—as some of those who cry out against his "betrayal" of existentialism do forget —that the products of analysis are not foundational. Sartre does not forget that analytical reason is but a moment of dialectical reason any more than he appeals to unreason as the source from which one may supply that which analytical reason cannot provide. When Heidegger came to the end of analytical reason, when Jaspers came to shipwreck, both looked beyond to a ground or source in which or from which one might draw or receive that which reason could not yield, that which might "situate" reason, control its excesses, remove its seductive character. One need only say that in this, as in so much else, Sartre is not a prophetic existentialist.

The lines immediately above reveal the "delicacy" of the distinction which was alluded to earlier. In emphasizing the need to avoid reification without paying the price of asserting the occurrence of unique individuals, I have almost made it impossible to speak of any notion of "individual" which would be stronger than that of "part" or "instance" or, perhaps, "object." But it is Sartre who tells us that there is no history except that made by historical individuals. It is in and through the individual's grasp of the dialectic that the necessity of history is to be revealed. There is no necessity apart from an individual certification, but necessity is not "for him" in the sense in which people say that something is "true for me"—or not only so. There are those who say that a logical truth is a truth for every mind. The necessity of the historical dialectic is not this. It is often said that a claim made on the basis of experiment must be capable of being certified by any competent observer. The qualification "competent" severely restricts the seriousness of this variety of intersubjectivity, but, even if one neglects this, the intent of the imposition of this methodological procedure is to minimize or eliminate subjectivity. What holds despite the individual peculiarities of the observers is—almost by definition—"objective" in the sense of being independent of individual wish, whim, or frailty. To then add that what thus obtains is a grasp of what is "objective" in the sense of being "in the world" or in "reality" is a bit startling, since what is peculiar to no given individual might well be that which is common to all, whether there be an "external" world or not. There are idealists. But no matter. The difficulties of realists is not our subject here. The point is that even this variety of intersubjectivity is not an instance of the kind of grasp which dialectic must secure.

Why not? First, because dialectic can obtain no purchase in a world of naive realism, whether that realism be materialistic or not. It can obtain no grasp because that world is constituted in such a way as to forbid a grasp which is not ultimately contemplative, an apprehension which Sartre would say is avail-

152

able only to deity. Second, because the dialectician does not grasp the objective *because* he is competent, but is competent *because* he grasps. But the term which should have been used is not "grasp," but "posit" or "reveal" or some other term which suggests that the apprehension of dialectical necessity is itself "constructive" or "creative" or "revealing"—in short, is itself dialectical. But to say this is to say that the necessity of the transition from dialectical reason to analytical reason cannot be established apart from the act itself. Sartre's claim that dialectical reason necessarily degrades itself would be self-inconsistent if it were exhibited by himself or by another in analytical form. Does this mean that what we have here is just another version of the claim that one must believe before he can understand? Perhaps. It is certain that the attempt to assess a dialectical claim from a non-dialectical stance can result in nothing other than the display of those absurdities with which we have been regaled by a long line of Anglo-Saxon philosophers. But the difference between the kind of *commitment* dialectic requires and the kind that analytical techniques require is not as different as might be expected. Before one can use analytical reasoning, one must first construct a domain in which it can be used. The injunctions, "The first step is to state the problem," or, "Yes, the topic is very interesting but first we must cut it down to manageable proportions," have been repeated ad nauseum both in and out of the classroom. Before we can deal "scientifically" with the qualitative phenomena encountered in direct perception, we have to *measure*, we have to use *instruments*, in short, we have to commit ourselves to a method which generates a world. One is almost tempted to say with Kant that all analysis presupposes synthesis. But that rendering would fail to exhibit a fault built into the immediately preceding discussion, namely, that it is conducted in terms which suggest that we have two independent activities, the creation of the domain and the subsequent analysis thereof. As we noted earlier,

153

Sartre contends that these are aspects of a single act, that *part of* analytical reason is the creation of a *champ pratique.*

This inherence is nothing mysterious. A common illustration is found in saying that one who uses mathematical techniques "sees the field *as*" structured in a manner susceptible to mathematical treatment. One can well imagine that the field might be *lived* as having these structures so that one would *literally fail to see* that the field was not "given" but was "taken with difficulty." To a man who has worked at length in an analytical manner, there is no difficulty in neglecting the awareness that he *both* maintains the field and works in it simply by confining his attention to some kinds of problems and not others and to the "standard" techniques. After one teaches elementary logic for a bit, many things become "obvious" that were nothing of the kind when logic was first encountered. Nor are they obvious to all students. Many of them have yet to learn that there is no such thing as "reading over" an assignment in logic and no such thing as understanding logic but being unable to work the problems. What one has to say to a student of this kind is that he must commit himself to the performance of the activity, and only then will he understand. Does one guarantee that he will understand? Of course not. One guarantees that he will not understand unless he first commits himself and does the work. After he has done so, he may or may not understand. We'll find out on the final! But what have we here? Is the student being asked to believe before he understands? The notion seems ludicrous. Belief simply is not in point. It is merely commitment which is required. Very well. The dialectician asks no more.

The most recent portions of our discussion have included an emphasis which allows a reading which must be prevented, namely, that both analytical and dialectical reason carve out a domain through commitment, and operate within it. Do we then have the familiar circumstance which can be likened to

154

that in which we choose between bridge and poker? Sartre apparently thinks not. It was said above that the constitution of the domain was *part* of the activity called analytical reason. But what must be added is that this part is precisely the inherence of the analytical in the dialectical, that which makes the former but a moment in the latter. One is reminded of Kant's view of the relation between *Vernunft* and *Verstand* where the understanding is sometimes said to be reason "under the title" of the understanding. Because reason, like reflection or like consciousness, is intentionally related to its "object," because all such activities are clarifications of an *action* already in progress, reason cannot help but objectify itself. The only question is in what manner it shall do so, that is, whether it shall posit a realm of the wholly definite, a realm amenable to the precise techniques of the "formal" disciplines or of those disciplines plus terms drawn from experience, or whether it shall embrace a logic of the not wholly definite. If the latter course were chosen, that "logic" would try to mold itself to a domain in which one experiences the "fluidification of everything stable" in which the thing itself would be left to develop itself in a field in which the dialectic of consciousness would become the consciousness of the dialectic.

To speak of this "choice" in the usual sense of the term would be mistaken in the manner suggested above and in this case it would be doubly mistaken. One may choose to make a field which is not wholly definite *more* definite, but the reverse seems impossible. Were we to have begun in a realm which was wholly definite, we would not have begun at all. The same must be said of a wholly indefinite realm. The establishment of a definite domain presupposes a field in which there are only partial orders. To make it more definite, one need not only *restrict* one's view, *select* some partial order, *focus* one's attention, but one must also *maintain* the selection through steady if not deliberate effort. Hence, the abundance of methodological

155

procedures which one encounters in formal and empirical inquiry. *One establishes explicit methods not only to facilitate the work but also to maintain the domain.* It is precisely the *absence* of such methodological procedures which leads the "tough minded" to regard the realm of dialectic as chaos or fraud. But the maintenance of such methods and, in consequence, the persistence of a firming of the not wholly definite is *an act in the realm of the nondefinite in terms of that realm.*

Notice that once one has committed himself to a fully structured field, it is false to say that the activity *within* that field is dialectical. If it is true that the very activity of making-definite will in time produce its contrary, then the activity might be said to be dialectical where it includes the creation and maintenance of the field. But the claim that this kind of transition *must* occur is made doubtful by the fact that it apparently has not occurred in all cases. It may be that logical empiricism through the logic of its own development became transmuted into analysis, but, as Sartre says, it is also true that Marxism has become arrested in its own development, so that Sartre will have to do existentialism until the impetus of Marxism is recovered. It would appear that both men and movements can become so immersed in their own definite creations that they become definite enough to be rigid. True, rigidity must be risked since dialectical procession requires that one attain to the "extreme" in order to surpass, but what lacks here is a demonstration that *dépassement* is inevitable. Can Sartre say that to certify the "progress" one must take the long view? Hegel had to posit the position of a universal mind. So, says Sartre, do naive materialists—wrongly. Thus, he cannot. Perhaps this difficulty results from Sartre's "failure" to accept Merleau-Ponty's recommendation that Sartre diminish his emphasis upon the negativity of subjectivity. Perhaps this means nothing more than that Sartre must take Hegel's claim that negation is a relation more seriously than he has. But, whatever the diagnosis, even if Sartre has shown the

156

necessity of the transition from dialectical to analytical reason, he has not shown that reason cannot become arrested in the analytical mode. Neither has he shown that the choice of any particular mode of commitment "follows" from the general structures of Being. Shall we say that this move is like choosing between gaming or playing no game at all? Sartre does not legislate. I suggest that he does not because he knows very well that the necessity of dialectic requires precisely the radical view of human freedom which Sartre holds and has always held. The necessity of the dialectic will not eliminate the contingency of being nor the freedom of the human reality which must live in and with that contingency—and for himself.

Conclusion

We have seen that an examination of the notion of dialectical reason, the philosophic core of Sartre's Marxism, shows that the work Sartre did in *CRD* not only permits, but requires, the inclusion of his radical conception of freedom. To a large extent, the rest of *CRD* consists of the concrete task of showing how that conception may be integrated with man's social being. No attempt has been made in these pages to detail that effort except as portions of it were relevant to our concern. The task of indicating the full scope of Sartre's attempt at integration has been begun by Desan and Laing, and we shall soon have more extended treatments by G. Varet and Klaus Hartmann. Perhaps we shall even be fortunate enough to have a translation, hopefully from someone as skilled as Hazel Barnes. Our main task here is more limited, namely, to show that the charge that Sartre's early thought is fundamentally inconsistent with his later efforts is simply mistaken. To conclude our task, we should like to restate our contention in a context less explicitly concerned with major themes in *CRD* than has been the case in the last few chapters. To do this, we shall make use of three devices. First, we shall introduce passages from "Materialism and Revolution," suggesting by that act alone that they might as well come at the end of Sartre's thought as at the beginning of the portion with which we have been concerned. Second, we shall cite some of the opinions of Sartre's friend and critic, Maurice Merleau-Ponty, opinions which support the interpretation we have offered. Kwant tells us that in his last years, after *CRD* was published, Merleau-Ponty still directed his criticism of Sartre to Sartre's position in *Being and Nothingness*.[1] Finally, I shall use both Merleau-Ponty and excerpts from "Materialism and Revolution" to introduce a sketch of a different overall perspective than that which Sartre's detractors have taken, a perspective which it is hoped will be more illuminating than that to which we have taken lengthy exception.

To begin, we reproduce three passages from "Materialism and Revolution," connecting them through juxtaposition although they are not thus connected in Sartre's text:

Thus freedom is to be discovered only in the act, and is one with the act; it forms the basis of the relations and interrelations that constitute the act's internal structures. It never derives pleasure from itself, but reveals itself in and through its results. It is not an inner virtue which permits us to detach ourselves from very pressing situations, because, for man, there is no inside and no outside. But it is, on the contrary, the power to commit one's self in present action and to build a future; it generates a future which enables us to understand and change the present.

Freedom is a structure of human action and appears only in commitment; determinism is the law of the world. And the act only calls for partial linkages and local constants. Similarly, it is not true that a free man cannot hope to be liberated. For he is not free and bound in respect to the same things. His freedom is like the illumination of the situation into which he is cast. But other people's freedoms can render his situation unbearable, drive him to rebellion or death.

160

A revolutionary philosophy ought to account for the plurality of free-doms and show how each one can be an object for the other while being, at the same time, a freedom for itself. Only this double character of freedom and objectivity can explain the complex notions of oppression, conflict, failure and violence. For one never oppresses anything but a freedom, but one cannot oppress it if it lends itself in some way to this oppression, if, that is, it presents the appearance of a thing to the Other. The revolutionary movement and its plan—which is to make society pass through the violence of one state in which liberties are alienated to another state based on their mutual recognition—is to be understood in these terms.[2]

The first excerpt shows clearly that Sartre's view of human freedom has long been exactly what it is now—there is no freedom apart from situation. As Merleau-Ponty has it, ". . . we are not body and spirit or consciousness *confronting* the world but spirit incarnate, being-in-the-world."[3] No doubt another selection of passages from *Being and Nothingness*, or the inclination to read that work from the point of view of some of Sartre's literary efforts, would permit the construction of a case for a freedom much less *engagé*. But the case we present indicates the contrary and thus blunts the criticism which is based upon a reading of Sartre which sees him as an advocate of an acosmic freedom. I know of no better epitome of the position we take than that written by Merleau-Ponty *in 1945* when speaking of the stance which both he and Sartre took:

. . . the merit of the new philosophy is precisely that it lies, in the notion of existence, to find a way of thinking about our condition. In the modern sense of the word "existence" is the movement through which man is in the world and involves himself in a physical and social situation which then becomes his point of view on the world. All involvement is ambiguous because it both affirms and restricts a freedom: . . .[4]

We fully agree with Merleau-Ponty that only the paradoxical assertion that involvement *both* affirms and restricts freedom does full justice to Sartre's thought.

Merleau-Ponty also understands that the adjective "social"

161

is of sufficient consequence to be made a member of the conjunction which modifies "situation." As the last line of the second excerpt from Sartre shows, the resistance, the threat, the restriction which is the Other is at least as weighty as the "coefficient of adversity" which is discovered in things. In *Being and Nothingness*, Sartre concentrated primarily upon an "individualistic" or "psychological" treatment of the Other. The second chapter in this book, "Freedom's Bonds," sketched some of that treatment. I suggest that *CRD* represents Sartre's further analysis of the individual, but now of the individual *as social*, perhaps even as the social being which Marx insisted he was. Because this book has been chiefly concerned with treating specifically "philosophical" themes, most of the detail of Sartre's "sociology" has been deliberately omitted. Our concern has been to show that *CRD* has in part spelled out many of the themes indicated in Sartre's earlier work, for instance, the theme of reciprocity announced in the first portion of the third excerpt above. This is not to deny that *CRD* is an independent synthesis but to contend that "development" is a much more appropriate term than "conversion" to describe the relationship between Sartre's early concerns and those of his latest massive work.

We can use the third excerpt from one more point although we say frankly that this usage is a tour de force. The first three lines of that quotation reveal the sinuosity which has led some to despair of being able to find argument in *CRD*. They reveal the "viscous" aspect which has long haunted Sartre's world. But the last line has a significantly different tone. It implies that the present version of the human predicament can be overcome even though one will have to pay the penalty of violence and the penalty of the further involvement of liberty in a field structured by alienation. This hint of "optimism" is indeed a tone of the whole essay from which the excerpt is taken. While Sartre makes it clear that he appreciates the difficulties of suc-

162

cessful revolution even to the point of entertaining the real possibility of its failure, the impression left is that his doubts are in no way an impediment to making the attempt, to "acting without hope." Men can, if they will, overcome the natural handicap of indolence and the intellectual handicap of the materialist myth so that socialism may arrive. But Sartre's concern in this essay is with whether or not socialism will be achieved, rather than with what might then ensue. In *Search for a Method*, we find him speaking at length of the "permanent" revolution and speaking of the time beyond the attainment of the classless society. These themes do not appear for the first time in *Search*, for, in 1955, Merleau-Ponty criticized Sartre sternly for advancing the first of them. But, between 1945 and 1960, Sartre shifted his attitude toward the possible success of the socialist revolution. It would not be difficult to point to events of that period which might well have led to reduced enthusiasm. It is tempting to speak of Sartre's almost pathetic delight in Castro's early efforts. We have already spoken of some of the disturbing factors in the situation in France in the late forties which led to Sartre's periodic estrangement from the Communist party, and events like these might well be cited as portents. But to proceed in this fashion would be curiously inappropriate when the man whose opinions are being explained has long maintained that a human's response to the deliverances of his experience is always free. It would be better to explain the retreat from enthusiasm by an increasing awareness on Sartre's part, of the weight of man's social being, an awareness brought to full force by the very writing of *CRD*. If thought is the self-clarification of action, we should prefer to have Sartre's action give rise to the new height of awareness. Were this line taken, one could then add that the development of the idea of permanent revolution might well be reinforced by the awareness of the increased risk that the socialist revolution might fail.

Both of these "explanations," however, smack of indulgence and assign an impact to Sartre's circumstances which verges on misrepresentation. To "explain" thusly is to entertain the belief that *CRD* expresses a crucial turning point in which Sartre must struggle to maintain the freedom of the individual against the forces and entanglements which his own analysis of the social has revealed. In other words, struggle on behalf of the individual, on behalf of freedom, is one of the tasks in which Sartre is now engaged. But the term which describes Sartre's efforts on behalf of individual autonomy is struggle, not abandonment. And one is immediately reminded that there is no realization of freedom apart from resistance. Only if one encounters the most fierce resistance could one expect to achieve the full revelation of freedom, and, if freedom is to encounter maximum resistance, freedom itself will have to generate that maximum. I suggest that Sartre has knowingly, deliberately thrust his cherished freedom into that aspect of the field in which it is in greatest peril *precisely in order to deepen the awareness that it is*. What is most at stake in the realm depicted in *CRD* is Sartre himself. A dialectician could do no less—if he had Sartre's savage courage. The human reality cannot be said to have emerged unscathed from peril in what we have of CRD. Without retracting an iota of our dissatisfaction with Sartre's detractors, we can nevertheless sympathize with their concern for the well-being of freedom. We do not say that one must agree with what Sartre has done, much less that one must follow him. But if we cannot follow Sartre's lead, we must surely watch carefully and with great interest this process which may be progress and which is certainly high drama.

164

Footnotes

Introduction

1. Mary Warnock, *The Philosophy of Sartre* (Hutchinson University Library, 1965), p. 135.
2. Ibid., p. 176.
3. Jean-Paul Sartre, *Search for a Method*, trans. H. Barnes (Knopf, 1963). Hereafter cited as *Search*.
4. Ibid., p. 33.
5. Jean-Paul Sartre, *Critique de la Raison Dialectique* (Gallimard, 1960). Hereafter cited as *CRD*.
6. *Search*, pp. 38-39.
7. Ibid., pp. 38-39.
8. Ibid., p. 34.
9. Ibid., p. 92.

Chapter 1

1. Jean-Paul Sartre, *Being and Nothingness*, trans. H. Barnes (Philosophical Library, 1956).
2. The essay, "Existentialism is a Humanism" is a result of such engagement.

The best translation of that essay is in W. Kaufmann, ed., *Existentialism from Dostoevesky to Sartre* (World Publishing Company, 1956), pp. 287-311.

3. Jean-Paul Sartre, "Materialism and Revolution" in *Sartre Literary and Philosophical Essays*, ed. A. Michelson (Collier Books, 1962), pp. 198-256.

4. Sartre, "Existentialism is a Humanism," p. 290.

5. Ibid., p. 291.

6. Ibid., p. 291.

7. Ibid., p. 303.

8. Ibid., pp. 291-293.

9. Ibid., pp. 307-308.

10. Maurice Merleau-Ponty, *Sense and Non-Sense*, trans. H. Dreyfus and P. Dreyfus (Northwestern University Press, 1964), p. 47.

11. Sartre, "Materialism and Revolution," p. 235.

12. Ibid., p. 225.

13. Ibid., p. 229.

14. Ibid., pp. 238-239.

15. Ibid., p. 249.

16. Ibid., p. 246.

17. Ibid., p. 242.

18. Ibid., p. 248.

19. Ibid., p. 243.

20. Ibid., p. 253.

Chapter 2

1. Adam Schaff, "Marxism and the Philosophy of Man" in *Socialist Humanism*, ed. E. Fromm (Doubleday, 1965), pp. 130-131.

2. *Being and Nothingness*, p. 482.

3. Ibid., p. 483 (Italics mine).

4. Jean-Paul Sartre, *The Transcendence of the Ego* (Noonday Press, 1957), p. 68.

5. See, for instance, G. Marcel, "Existence and Human Freedom" in *The Philosophy of Existentialism* (Citadel, 1966), pp. 49,53.

6. H. J. Blackham, *Six Existentialist Thinkers* (Harper, 1959), p. 115.

7. *Being and Nothingness*, p. 567.

Chapter 3

1. *CRD*, pp. 147-152.

2. For one who takes similar liberties with Sartre see Maurice Merleau-Ponty, *Les Aventures de al Dialectique* (Gallimard, 1955), pp. 138-139.

3. *CRD*, p. 124.
4. Ibid., p. 147.
5. Ibid., p. 147.
6. Ibid., p. 148.
7. Warnock's statement of this presumed shift is the most direct. See, for instance, *The Philosophy of Sartre*, pp. 177-178.
8. *CRD*, pp. 148-149.
9. Ibid., p. 150.
10. Ibid., p. 150.
11. Ibid., p. 151,
12. Ibid., p. 151.
13. Ibid., p. 151.
14. Ibid., p. 152.
15. For a powerful presentation of the claim and intuition and formalization are always linked, see Johnstone, pp. 105-122.
16. *CRD*, p. 152.

Chapter 4

1. *CRD*, pp. 166 ff.
2. Ibid., p. 167.
3. Ibid., p. 167.
4. Ibid., p. 168.
5. Ibid., p. 171.
6. Ibid., pp. 173-174.
7. Ibid., p. 175.
8. Ibid., p. 176.
9. Ibid., p. 180.
10. Ibid., p. 181.
11. Ibid., pp. 181-182.
12. Ibid., p. 182.
13. Ibid., p. 183.
14. Ibid., p. 183.
15. Ibid., p. 184.
16. Ibid., p. 184.
17. Ibid., p. 186.
18. Ibid., p. 192.
19. Ibid., p. 194.
20. Ibid., p. 194.
21. Ibid., p. 195.

22. Ibid., p. 196.
23. Ibid., p. 197.
24. Ibid., p. 197.
25. Ibid., p. 198.

Chapter 5

1. *CRD*, p. 750.

Conclusion

1. Remy C. Kwant, *From Phenomenology to Metaphysics* (Duquesne University Press, 1966), pp. 131-132.
2. Sartre, "Materialism and Revolution," pp. 243, 244, 251.
3. Merleau-Ponty, *Sense and Non-Sense*, p. 75.
4. *Ibid.*, p. 72.